Also by Chette Williams

HARD FIGHTING SOLDIER

Finding God in Trials, Tragedies, and Triumphs

THE
BROKEN
ROAD

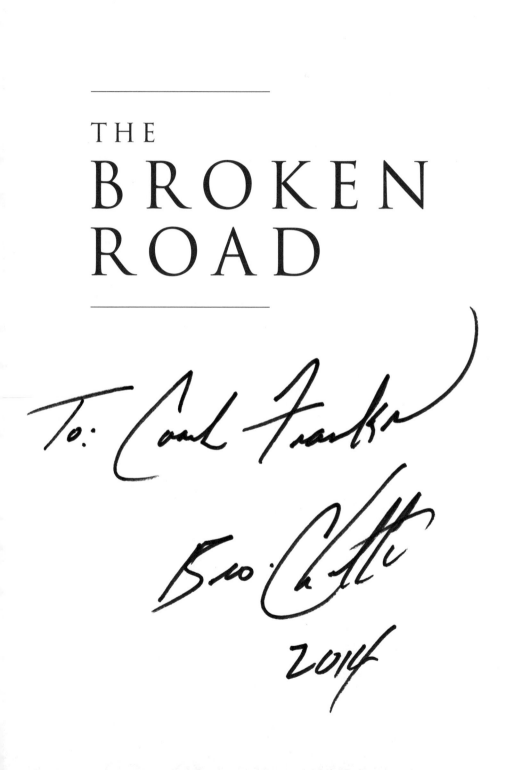

To: Coach Franks

Bro. Cattle

2014

THE
BROKEN
ROAD

Finding God's Strength and Grace
on a Journey of Faith

Chette Williams

CHAPLAIN, AUBURN UNIVERSITY FOOTBALL TEAM

LOOKING GLASS BOOKS

Published by
Looking Glass Books, Inc.
Decatur, Georgia

Distributed by John Blair, Publisher
Winston-Salem, North Carolina

Written in collaboration with Dick Parker

Book and cover design by Burtch Hunter Design

Manufactured in the United States

ISBN 978-1-929619-42-9

The audio version of *The Broken Road* is available at Audible.com.

Contact Rev. Chette Williams at CWilliams@fca.org.

Every life and every season, even a national championship
season, is a broken road where Christ walks with us,
comforts us, and offers us the opportunity to
comfort others on their broken road.

He comes alongside us when we go through hard times, and
before you know it, he brings us alongside someone else who is
going through hard times so that we can be there for that person just as God was there for us. Your hard times are also our
hard times. When we see that you're just as willing to endure
the hard times as to enjoy the good times, we know you're going
to make it, no doubt about it.

2 CORINTHIANS 1:4, 7 (THE MESSAGE)

GRATITUDE

Three Auburn University head football coaches have made our ministry possible. In 1999 Tommy Tuberville saw the need for a full-time chaplain dedicated to his players and assistant coaches, and he invited me to return to Auburn and fill that role. Ten years later, Gene Chizik took our ministry to a new level with his amazing support. And now Gus Malzahn is totally committed to our work at Auburn. As we begin our fifteenth season, I am grateful to each of these men, and especially to God for the incredible opportunities He has offered.

Two Auburn athletic directors, David Housel and Jay Jacobs, supported the coaches in their decision to invite me to Auburn and to continue our work. Jay and David also had a direct hand in the creation of this book. Jay generously shared his personal story. David, who understands the heart of Auburn as well as any living soul, guided us at critical points in the creation of the manuscript.

Hundreds of football players and their coaches have opened their hearts and allowed us to share with them the love of Christ, and I am grateful for them. We would not be able to reach any of those players without the prayers and financial generosity of many, many supporters. Thank you.

I am thankful for my mother, who showed me the right path from the beginning.

And I am especially grateful to God for my wife, Lakeba, whose love gives me strength to travel this broken road. My responsibilities to the team often take me away from Lakeba and our children, and they have been immensely patient with me through the years. My love for them knows no limit.

To you, the reader, thank you for reading our story and sharing this experience with me as we travel the road together.

CONTENTS

THE
BROKEN
ROAD

JOY MEETS SORROW
ON THE ROAD

OCTOBER 16, 2010

CRAIG STEVENS AND Mike Blanc hit the Arkansas runner hard. The ball popped out and wobbled slowly, as if it had been nudged across the grass toward safety Zac Etheridge. Zac reached down, swept it up, then turned and sprinted toward the goal line forty-seven yards away. For the next few seconds the whole world seemed to move out of Zac's way. Teammates Nick Fairley, Daren Bates, and Neiko Thorpe followed, looking for somebody to block, but not a single Arkansas player was close enough to lay a hand on Zac. The road had already been cleared.

Thousands of people in the stands and everybody on the Auburn sideline jumped and cheered and laughed. Some were shedding tears. They understood the significance of Zac's run went way beyond the eight-point lead and the momentum it created. Zac's touchdown was life changing. A year earlier, after a crushing hit, Zac had fallen motionless near midfield, paralyzed from the neck down for several long, silent minutes. He was carefully placed on a stretcher, immobilized, and carried off the field. We wondered that day if Zac would walk again. Now, he was racing toward his first-ever Auburn touchdown.

It was one of those moments when it seems like the hand of God has reached down and altered our course. Thousands of years ago, He promised, "I will repay you for the years the locusts have eaten." This was payback time for Zac. Payback for the fear. Payback for the weeks he had to wear that big neck brace. Payback for the months in rehab.

Zac high-stepped across the goal line, and Nick immediately jumped on his back in celebration. (Zac's mother, up in the stands, probably shuddered when our playful three-hundred-pound defensive lineman bounded toward her son.) Zac tossed the ball to the referee and trotted toward the sideline, where just about everybody was laughing and jumping with joy. Except Zac didn't see Aairon. Where was Aairon?

Aairon Savage was like a brother to Zac. For five years they had practiced together in the defensive backfield, trained together, prayed together, rehabbed injuries together. Aairon had missed two full seasons with major injuries and surgeries. Almost three years passed from his last game in 2007 until his first game in 2010—years of grueling training with no promise that he would ever play again. Because of his injuries, the NCAA had given Aairon one more opportunity to play, and in seven games he had stood out as a leader on defense.

Aairon and Zac had begun this play, like so many others, side-by-side in their safety positions, behind the linebackers. Zac thought Aairon would have been the first to congratulate him when he crossed the goal line. That he would have beaten Nick to the end zone.

But just as Zac had reached down to pick up the football near midfield, Aairon was hit and went down near the spot where Zac's spine had been fractured a year earlier, his right leg broken. While the entire stadium watched Zac cross the goal line, Aairon was lying in pain.

The excitement on the sideline settled, and the extra-point team ran onto the field, but Zac still hadn't found Aairon. Finally he turned and saw the trainers gathered near midfield and Coach Gene Chizik walking toward them. It took only a moment for Zac to realize they were talking to Aairon, who was still wearing his helmet, and then they were helping him to stand on his left foot, anguish in his face. Instantly, Zac's joy was gone. His shoulders slumped, and he swung his helmet at his side in frustration. He knew that Aairon might be coming off the field for the final time as an Auburn player.

He walked out to comfort his brother, and if he could have turned back the clock just two minutes, he would have gladly given back his only touchdown for Aairon to have two healthy legs. He touched the top of Aairon's helmet, then turned to walk back to the sideline. Zac's touchdown had given Auburn an eight-point lead, but none of the players were celebrating or even smiling anymore. Instead, guys were sitting in small groups, many with their heads down, some crying in frustration.

You may already know the end of this story—how Wes Byrum kicked a field goal for Auburn as time expired to beat Oregon 22–19. How confetti fell from the ceiling and tears of joy streamed as Coach Chizik raised the crystal football national championship trophy. You may have read or watched television specials about Auburn's "road to the championship"—the overtime win against Clemson, Cam Newton's amazing run against LSU, and the come-from-behind win at Tuscaloosa.

Let me tell you something else about that road to the championship. It is a broken road. For all the joy we experienced, we also knew injuries and sorrows and disappointments. Players endured pain and witnessed the suffering of others along the way. Yet isn't that the nature of every journey? Every season? Every life? We all travel a broken road. Even in our journey to Him, God allows us to bear pain and heartache almost to the breaking point, because those experiences strengthen us. They open our eyes to the hardships of people around us so we can be a comfort to them. They remind us that our strength comes from God.

God honors the broken road in the gospel accounts, which are filled with transformations that occurred on broken roads. The good Samaritan encountered and then cared for a man who had been attacked on the winding mountain road to

Nobody really knew what was going on with Aairon when he went down. We didn't know if he had cramped up or what. We just knew he was injured. Then we saw him take his helmet off, and the tears in eyes, and we knew something terrible was going on—that this was his final play after a great career as a college football player, coming back from injury after injury and showing so much courage. Aairon is the epitome of what a college athlete should be.

RYAN PUGH
OFFENSIVE LINEMAN

Jericho. A father looked up to see his wayward son returning home, and he ran out to embrace him on the road. The blind beggar Bartimaeus received his sight on the road to Jericho.

Jesus was born on the road, after his parents had traveled eighty miles down a dusty trail to Bethlehem, and He died by the side of a broken road, nailed to a cross on Golgotha. Three days later, two of His followers were walking on the road to Emmaus, dejected, when the risen Christ came alongside them, visited with them, and warmed their hearts.

Brutality and tender care. Ruin and compassion. Blindness and sight. Agony and mercy. The broken road transforms us long before we reach our destination.

Players and coaches look at the championship ring on their finger and remember a night in Arizona when they became national champions. My prayer for them is that they remember the journey more than the moment, the pain and the mercy more than the confetti.

In this book I have collected stories of that journey to help them remember and to share with others a few of the trials they faced and the places where God met them along the way.

The journey began years before the 2010 team had come together.

SEEKING
GOD'S FAVOR

DECEMBER 2004

P EACE, THE ANGELS declared at the first Christmas.

But Christmastime in the Auburn Athletic Complex is rarely peaceful. In the best of times, coaches and support staff are packing and preparing to travel to a bowl game hundreds of miles away, where they may celebrate Christmas with their families in a hotel. In the worst of times, they're wondering if they'll have a job come New Year's Day.

Three days before Christmas 2004, there was peace in Auburn. On that cool, clear Wednesday morning, students had gone home, downtown was nearly deserted, and our town's version of a white Christmas was the hundreds of bits of toilet paper still fluttering in the oak trees at Toomer's Corner after twelve straight game-winning celebrations.

Across campus, the football players had finished their final practice before going home to spend Christmas with their families. The team was undefeated. They had won the Southeastern Conference championship and were ranked third best in the nation. Peace.

Upstairs in the Athletic Complex that afternoon, Jay Jacobs was introduced as Auburn's new athletic director. Jay had been my teammate at Auburn twenty-one years earlier. Like me, he was a walk-on with no scholarship. He was not quite big enough to be recruited to play offensive tackle, his position. He came to Auburn anyway because he loved it, and his hard work on the practice field and in the weight room earned him a starting position. Jay was strong as a bull. He also had a mischievous streak. (One night when we were students, he and I created fake passes and worked security at a concert on campus.) Like me, Jay had a life-changing encounter at Auburn and committed his life to Christ.

Reading his Bible several days before his appointment as athletic director, Jay had come across Proverbs 29:26: "Many seek the ruler's favor, but justice for man comes from the Lord."

He read the words again: "Many seek the ruler's favor."

Jay, in his humility, never considered himself a ruler, although many would soon seek his favor. Instead, he thought about how a university athletic director might seek favor from numerous "rulers": the board of trustees, the university president, generous donors, alumni, fans, and even the media. He vowed in his heart to live instead by the statement, *but justice for man comes from the*

Lord. Or as Jesus said in the Sermon on the Mount, "Seek first the kingdom of God and His righteousness, and all these things shall be added to you."

"We get caught up in the competitiveness and the winning," Jay says, "and it really can impact your mind-set. Any place can be as dark or as light as you want it to be. We all fight our spiritual battles. We're called to shine light in the dark places, whether we're in athletics, academics, a Fortune 500 company, or a sole-proprietorship business.

"My prayer this morning was, 'God, transform my mind so I can begin to think a new way, not the old way,' which is something I have to constantly remind myself."

Me too. Constantly.

On December 22, 2004, surrounded by media, family, and friends, Jay stood at the podium and quoted Proverbs 29:26, and he said his approach would be based on its truth. He had no idea where that commitment would lead him or how it would challenge him.

A COMFORTER

FEBRUARY 2007

J ERRAUD POWERS, a rising sophomore defensive back, underwent shoulder surgery in Birmingham in February 2007. Andrew McCain, who had been in Jerraud's recruiting class, called his mother and asked if she could stop by St. Vincent's Hospital, just a few miles from their home, and check on his teammate.

Laurie McCain knew Jerraud well. "Our whole signing class was close," Jerraud says, "from the first guy to the twenty-sixth. You form a bond growing up together. And whenever our parents came to town, we'd introduce them to the other guys. They all took responsibility for us. In fact, my mother still gets mad at Sen'Derrick Marks if he doesn't stop in Decatur and let her cook a meal for him when he's on his way to Nashville. Same with Aairon's mom. If I'm anywhere close to Albany, she expects to see me."

Six weeks before Jerraud's surgery, he and a dozen other guys had piled into the McCains' RV with Laurie and Kyle and ridden with them to Dallas for the Cotton Bowl game against Nebraska. (Players arrange their own transportation to and from bowl games.) So it's not an understatement to say they felt like family when they got back home.

When Andrew told Laurie about Jerraud's surgery, she baked a batch of cookies and put them in a basket to carry to the hospital, then she bought a card and wrote a note. She knocked on the hospital room door, and Jerraud's mother invited her in.

"Andrew's mom sat there in the room with us and talked to me as if I were her own son," Jerraud remembers. "She told my mom and me that we could call her if we needed anything at all."

Laurie looked at Jerraud and imagined her own son stretched out on a gurney far away ("Those boys look so big hanging off those little tables," she says), being rolled into the operating room, and wondered what it would be like if she couldn't be with him. She stayed until Jerraud fell asleep, then she went home, knowing this wouldn't be her last hospital visit. She called Andrew and asked him to let her know when other players might need encouragement. God was calling her into a ministry of comfort.

I lost count of the number of players I've stood by and kneeled with in hospital emergency rooms. So many broken bones, dislocated shoulders, torn-up knees, ripped Achilles tendons, cracked vertebrae, and concussions. I've prayed with my friends as they were carried off the field, knowing they had reached the end of this road, their football careers and their dreams finished. I've held their hands in hospitals while they waited for their parents to arrive.

Pain, which is often accompanied by loss, is a lonely, scary place. We need someone to walk with us and encourage us as we live through it.

Too often I cannot be with every player for every hospital visit. Surgery is often scheduled in Birmingham (a hundred miles north of Auburn) or Pensacola (two hundred miles to the south), where Dr. James Andrews, our team orthopedic surgeon, practices. Sometimes parents can't come either, because they don't have the financial means to leave their jobs and families to spend a day or more in the hospital with their sons. So I call the players in their hospital rooms, and their teammates and coaches call. We talk with them and pray with them and try to cheer them up. Then we hang up the phone, and they're alone again.

When Jerraud was discharged from the hospital, his mother asked him to come home to Decatur for a few days, but he wanted to get back to Auburn. "I think Mom was more comfortable letting me go back to Auburn, knowing that the McCains were looking out for me like I was their son," he says. "She didn't have to worry about anything. Otherwise, she would have followed me back to Auburn."

A week later, Laurie sent Jerraud a card and cookies and

another card a week after that. When spring practice started, Jerraud wasn't able to go full contact. Andrew told his mother that Jerraud was struggling with his rehab, and she called to encourage him. "I wanted to make sure he knew that God has a plan for him," Laurie says. "That what Satan intends for evil, God intends for good."

Andrew had told Laurie about other players who were struggling through the summer away from their families, and she sent notes and cookies to them. One teammate described her "like a room mom in second grade, just making people feel better."

When Jesus promised, "I will pray the Father, and he shall give you another Comforter," He was talking about the Holy Spirit, who works in and through real people like Laurie McCain to come alongside us in our journey.

Players go through trying times, especially in summer when we'd normally be at home but instead we're training, away from our families. Or during Christmas break when other students go home, we stay to practice, except for a couple of days. You miss a lot of holidays.

Then you get notes in the mail. After a workout I'd get a couple of envelopes with notes from moms telling me they were thinking about me or praying for me. Just that little thing that boosts our confidence and reminds us that there's something out there that's bigger than football—a group of moms praying for our safety, well-being, and spiritual guidance.

RYAN PUGH

NOT WANTED

SEPTEMBER 2007

ANDREW MCCAIN CAME to Auburn in 2005 as a tight end and defensive end. He played five games at defensive tackle his freshman year, then after the season the coaches asked him to consider a move to offensive line. Andrew agreed and spent his sophomore year as a redshirt, delaying a year of eligibility by not playing in any games. Over the months, he prepared for the move by working out with strength and conditioning coach Kevin Yoxall (known to the players as Coach Yox) and adding fifty pounds to his frame. Andrew just wanted to play—offense or defense, tight end or tackle, right or left.

By spring 2007 Andrew weighed nearly three hundred pounds. He had moved to the top of the depth chart at right tackle, and the coaches named him the most improved offensive lineman. The o-line coach told the media, however, that he wasn't satisfied with the offensive line play, and when freshman tackle Lee Ziemba arrived on campus that summer, within a week of practice he had risen to the top of the depth chart. Andrew was moved to the left side of the line, where he played backup to senior tackle King Dunlap.

The season opened with high expectations. We had won eleven games in 2006 and finished the season ranked ninth in the nation. Yet in the first game of 2007 against Kansas State, we trailed for most of the second half, and our home crowd grew increasingly restless. We finally took the lead with two minutes left and won the game.

A week later on Saturday night, our guys struggled again for most of the game against South Florida—three fumbles and two interceptions. South Florida kicked a field goal to tie the game with a minute left and send it to overtime, then somewhere close to midnight they scored a touchdown to win. After the game we gathered players from both teams on the field for a prayer, like we always do, and I couldn't remember Jordan-Hare Stadium ever being as quiet. All we could hear was murmuring as the disappointed crowd trudged to the exits.

Mississippi State came to Auburn the third week of the season, and nothing went right. The crowd was already impatient at the opening kickoff, then Mississippi State drove to our fifteen-yard line and kicked a field goal. We got the ball going the other direction, and the first time our senior quarterback, Brandon

Cox, passed, Derek Pegues intercepted and ran it back for a touchdown. Seven minutes into the game we trailed 10–0, and the boos were starting up. Some guy sitting right behind our bench was yelling for Coach Tuberville to put in Kodi Burns, our five-star freshman quarterback. We got the ball again, and Brandon went back onto the field with the offense. His next pass was intercepted, and the boos rained down loudly as Brandon jogged toward the sideline. Thousands of people—Auburn people in our home stadium—booed Brandon.

I usually don't spend time with players during games, because they need to get their instructions from the coaches, but I ran over to Brandon and put my arms around him. I wanted to cover his ears and protect him from this moment. I wanted to yell into the stands and remind the people that this was the man who played through awful pain almost every day of the 2006 season. Two LSU defensive linemen had sacked him violently and injured his ankle and knee, and for much of the season he had to take off his boot cast to play on Saturday—and still he led the team to eleven wins. This was the man who had been diagnosed in high school with myasthenia gravis, a rare neuromuscular disease, and he never used it as an excuse. He didn't even tell his Auburn teammates about his condition until his junior year.

Now Brandon had made a mistake—he had thrown a couple of interceptions—and he needed a safe place to come to. But his own people were turning on him. I know it happens at other places, but I hate when Auburn people do it. I imagined Jesus telling the story of the prodigal son and changing the ending. The son comes over the final hill and is in sight of home, shoulders slumped, feet dragging, knowing he deserves nothing and praying only for his father's mercy. But instead of greeting him with compassion, the father runs out of the house and chases him off with a stick. "Git, boy! Git out of here! Boo!" That's what I heard our people saying to Brandon. It was one of the sickest feelings I've ever experienced. And it wasn't the first time I'd seen it happen. Ben Leard and Jason Campbell and Daniel Cobb and later Chris Todd, all of them Auburn quarterbacks, all of them good men, were booed at Auburn. I saw those guys broken and ready to walk off the field, abandoned in the place they called home.

When we got the ball back, Coach Tuberville sent Kodi in at quarterback, and the crowd exploded in cheers. I wondered if Brandon remembered the first time he had been on the receiving end of those cheers. Three years earlier, coaches had told Jason Campbell, our senior quarterback, that he would have to share snaps with Brandon, who was just a redshirt freshman. In the first game against Louisiana-Monroe, the crowd had cheered when Brandon, the new kid, ran onto the field to start the second quarter. They cheered even louder that day when Brandon drove the offense seventy-one yards for a touchdown.

Now Brandon was a senior, standing on the sideline, and the cheers were for the freshman running onto the field. They were for Kodi.

A MOTHER'S PRAYERS

SEPTEMBER 15, 2007

I N THE STANDS at the Mississippi State game, Laurie and Kyle McCain watched the Auburn offense drive fifty yards until Kodi Burns was sacked from behind, the ball was knocked loose, and Mississippi State recovered. As our guys came off the field, King Dunlap, our starting left tackle, was holding his elbow. Through binoculars, Kyle watched King talking with the trainers and wondered if Andrew might get a chance to play.

On the next offensive series, Andrew took King's place on the offensive line. He played the rest of the game at left tackle, except for extra points, when King went back in.

Andrew took advantage of the opportunity, and on Sunday

afternoon he called to tell his parents that when the coaches reviewed the game video, he had graded out second highest among the offensive linemen. It looked like he would be starting against New Mexico State. They could almost hear his smile over the phone.

Two hours after Andrew's first Sunday call, Laurie and Kyle were sitting in evening church when Kyle's phone vibrated. It was a text from Andrew: "Call me right now." Knowing practice had just finished and fearing Andrew might have been injured, Kyle looked at Laurie and hurried outside to call. Andrew told his father he wouldn't be starting after all. The coaches had told him that freshman Ryan Pugh would start instead at left tackle. Andrew was angry, frustrated, and confused. Laurie hurt for her son, and Kyle reminded her that coaches have to make difficult decisions. But he was frustrated too.

Ryan wouldn't be the only freshman starting his first game against New Mexico State. Kodi Burns was named starting quarterback ahead of Brandon Cox.

College football players try to protect their parents from the realities of injuries, competition for starting positions, and issues with coaches. But parents, especially moms, know. They hear the pain through the telephone line. They read the speculations in the newspaper and hear them on the radio or from their friends.

Walking out of church on Sunday night, Laurie thought about Andrew and also about Brandon, who had been our starting quarterback since his sophomore season, and King, who had started every game at tackle since the beginning of 2006. She wondered how Brandon's mom, Debbie, was dealing with her son's disappointment, or King's parents up in Nashville. She heard the boos again in her mind, and she wanted to do more than just send a card to the players. Laurie believed in the power of prayer, and she wanted to bring together the mothers of other players on the team to pray for their sons and coaches. On Monday she called me and asked if I could find a place for the moms to meet before the game on Saturday. I checked and reserved a room for them in the Athletic Complex, and she got on the phone and put out the invitation.

Laurie's call to me was not unusual. In fact, I get a lot more calls from parents than players. Players text me or drop by my office. We visit in the parking lot outside the Athletic Complex, or they holler at me before or after practice. Parents call, usually when they haven't heard from their sons for a while. They're worried, and they want me to reassure them that all is well.

Sometimes calls come completely out of the blue from desperate parents. One morning that week, I answered the phone, and the man on the other end began by apologizing. He didn't have a son on the football team, but his daughter was a student at Auburn, and he hadn't heard from her in almost a month. She had been a good girl in high school, president of her youth group, and a great student. But something had changed. He had heard she was running with a fast crowd at Auburn. Her roommate hadn't seen her. Would I try to find her and ask her to call home? Would I tell her that her father loved her? Would I pray with him?

The young girl was lost. Lost and afraid. Like so many college kids, she had made some bad decisions. Now she felt alone in a dark place, afraid to tell her parents—afraid they might reject her.

Rejection is one of the greatest fears among college students. I assured the father that I would look for his daughter.

Brandon came to my office on Monday morning, and we talked and prayed together for a long time. Nobody I know has devoted more to Auburn football than Brandon Cox. Throughout his career he played through the disease that often left him weak and fatigued, and in his first two years as starting quarterback, Auburn won nineteen games. Now, three games into his senior season, Brandon had been replaced by a freshman, and he felt rejected. It would be a long week until Saturday.

Over those days Brandon, Andrew, and King worked as hard as ever at practice. In fact, practice is about the best place for a player to be when he has been replaced at the top of the depth chart. Running drills, throwing passes, blocking, and tackling are the things they know and do best. The hardest time is in the meeting room or the dining room or a teammate's living room. The guys who have lost their positions try to interact and hang out with their friends, and then they start to feel resentment, especially when a freshman has taken their position. They can see the younger guy's point of view—they walked into a situation and did exactly what you would do in the same circumstance. Every player on the team is here to play, the sooner the better. The older guys try to lay aside all those frustrations and any animosity. Jealousy only damages relationships and creates problems in the team. So they withdraw. Like the daughter of the man who called me, they find their own ways to cope with rejection.

"I think there comes a point in your life when you realize what it's like to be an adult," Andrew says now, "especially for athletes, who have such a different experience from the average college student. We have a lot of responsibility. A lot of accountability. You work hard to achieve good results, but sometimes the results are not so good. You handle more things on your own."

Later in the week I found the daughter. She reunited with her parents, and they came alongside her on her broken road.

I tell players that handling problems on your own is not the same as going it alone. I'm here to help. Coaches want to help. Teammates, and most of all, moms and dads want to help. The player says he understands. Then he walks away. Alone.

MOUNTAINTOPS
AND VALLEYS

SEPTEMBER 22, 2007

S ATURDAY CAME AND twenty-five mothers gathered in
the Athletic Complex to pray. Laurie was hoping for a
mountaintop experience, but too many of the moms cried in
frustration and disappointment for their sons who had lost
their starting positions. Other moms avoided eye contact,
hiding their excitement and pride for their sons who had
taken their places.

"It was hard," Sandra Pugh remembers. "My son took
Laurie's son's starting spot, and I thought it might not be a good
idea for me to sit with his mom in a prayer meeting. I didn't
know how she might feel about me, or if her son was upset with
mine." But Sandra went, and she prayed. One mom prayed for

a "tidal wave of revival" and reminded the group that they were God's family first, and He could bring them together as one. Another read 1 Corinthians 12:25–26 (NKJV):

> THERE SHOULD BE NO SCHISM IN THE BODY,
> BUT THAT THE MEMBERS SHOULD HAVE THE SAME CARE
> FOR ONE ANOTHER. AND IF ONE MEMBER SUFFERS,
> ALL THE MEMBERS SUFFER WITH IT; OR IF ONE MEMBER
> IS HONORED, ALL THE MEMBERS REJOICE WITH IT.

Other prayers were offered and some tears were shed. Then they said their amens and walked outside to cheer for their sons and the team as they walked down Donahue Drive to the stadium, a longtime Auburn tradition called Tiger Walk. On that fourth Saturday of the 2007 season, there had been no mountaintop experience for the mothers. But the good news of the biblical mountaintop is that Jesus didn't send the disciples away alone. He accompanied them down the mountain and into the valley. Laurie prayed for Jesus to be present, then walked out into the crowd.

Tiger Walk is a joyful time every home game for the players and coaches. Two hours before kickoff, they walk single file for about a quarter mile down a hill to the stadium entrance through a crowd of thousands of fans who cheer, call their names, and reach out to touch them. Every player is a star. Even the guys who have little hope of playing a single down feel the love. There are no hisses or boos. It's a brand-new day and a transforming moment. "We love you, Brandon!" they shout. "We believe in you, King!" Players come into the locker room so loved, so affirmed, so pumped up, I wish they could walk straight onto the field and play the game.

Imagine how we might change the world if we affirmed each other every day. If teachers lined up at the schoolhouse door and high-fived every student coming in. "You rock, Caitlyn!" Or if bosses cheered employees every morning. Then suppose we kept up the cheers and the affirmations all day long.

The moms had the right idea. When we start the day by praying for others, we almost always encounter opportunities to offer encouragement.

A SPIRIT THAT
IS NOT AFRAID

SEPTEMBER 29, 2007

AUBURN FANS AND the media got caught up in the "youth movement" of 2007, especially on the offensive line. Freshmen Lee Ziemba and Mike Berry started the first three games, then Chaz Ramsey replaced Mike, and Ryan Pugh started at tackle in the fourth game. None of the four had ever played a down in college before their first starts. There was no easing into their positions. They laughed sometimes that they didn't always know who to hit, but they hit somebody. Theirs was a surprising boldness—surprising because they were so young yet so unafraid of the moment, as if they saw none of the obstacles in their path. They reminded me of a line in the Auburn Creed: "I believe in . . . a spirit that is not afraid."

We beat New Mexico State 55–20, and a week later went to Gainesville for our first road game—against Tim Tebow and Florida, the third-ranked team in the nation and defending national champions, on Saturday night. Nobody gave us much of a chance.

Down in Florida they call Ben Hill Griffin Stadium "the Swamp." Head coach Urban Meyer had never lost a game there. But with less than four minutes left, the game was tied 17–17, and we had the ball with a chance to drive down for the win. Brandon Cox, who had won back his starting job, completed two passes on the drive, and Ben Tate ran again and again.

Then we saw the definition of *bold*.

With three seconds left in the game and the stadium rocking from the noise, Coach Tuberville called time-out and sent in our freshman kicker to win the game with a forty-three-yard field goal.

Wes Byrum, who was from Fort Lauderdale, didn't need anybody to tell him what his kick would mean. It was a heavy burden for an eighteen year old to bear. He ran onto the field and studied the spot where Matthew Motley would place the ball for him to kick. None of us could see Coach Meyer across the field with his hand resting lightly on a referee's shoulder. The crowd somehow yelled louder. The snap was perfect, the ball went down, and Wes kicked it straight through. Our guys ran onto the field, jumping and celebrating, and the Florida crowd fell silent. Until we saw the referee waving his arms. Apparently, right before the snap, Meyer had squeezed the referee's shoulder and said, "Now." The referee had blown his whistle and called time-out, but nobody had heard or seen—our eyes were on the ball. So the kick didn't count.

That was Meyer's attempt to "ice" Wes Byrum—to avoid losing his first home game ever at Florida. Wes, playing just his fifth college football game, looked toward the Florida bench, then he went back to the center of the field, eyed the spot where Matthew would place the ball for the second time, looked up at the goalpost, and focused on his spot once more. The ball was snapped and placed, and Wes kicked it again. Perfect.

That was bold. It's the kind of boldness that I, as a Christian, wish I could take into every situation. "I don't know what else goes on when I run onto the field," Wes says. "It's weird. I don't hear anything when I walk out there, especially when it's near the end of the game. I don't see anything in the crowd. I don't hear anything. I just see my spot [where the holder will place the ball] and the uprights."

WOUNDED
HEALERS

OCTOBER 6, 2007

L AURIE McCAIN COULD barely keep up with the cards and cookies. As soon as she mailed a batch to Auburn, Andrew called to tell her about another hurting player. Tray Blackmon, Merrill Johnson, Aairon Savage, and Jonathan Wilhite had all been injured. And that was just the defense. Every time she sealed a box of cookies, she prayed for the player and his family, that God would ease their worries.

Our home game against Vanderbilt was coming up, and she made plans for another prayer time with the moms. She hoped the wins against New Mexico State and Florida would ease the tension the mothers had expressed the first time they met and that they could lift each other up on Saturday morning.

The meeting location had been moved to Sewell Hall, where the players would be arriving in buses at 9:30 a.m. to begin Tiger Walk. Laurie walked up the hill toward Sewell, and the morning was so quiet. Overnight tailgaters were cooking breakfast or setting up grills. She walked into the old dorm at 7:30, half an hour ahead of the other mothers so she could be there to greet them. She stepped into the tired lobby with its worn carpet and poster-size photographs of Pat Sullivan and Bo Jackson, and she wondered if it had been updated since she was a student. She found the room we had reserved for them and arranged the chairs in a circle for the moms. Then she sat and waited.

For three decades, until the NCAA eliminated athletic dorms, game-day mornings in Sewell had been the center of our universe. Players ate the pregame meal, met with coaches for a final time, and walked out the door and down to the stadium. Sewell was my home for four years. It was the place where I grew up and the place where I came to Christ. It had been home to two Heisman Trophy winners, dozens of All-Americans, and Olympic champions. Then players moved out to dorms and apartments around town. The coaching staff needed to bring the team together on the night before games, so they began staying in a nearby hotel and coming back to campus on buses. On that Saturday morning in 2007, before the buses arrived, Sewell Hall was very quiet.

At 7:55 Laurie was still sitting by herself. Nobody was coming. She could feel it. She also felt confused. Wasn't this what God wanted her to do, to bring the mothers together to pray for their sons? Where were the others? At eight o'clock she prayed, "God, I thought You were gathering us together and teaching me to rejoice with my sisters." She waited a few more minutes, cried a bit, felt rejected and a little sorry for herself, asked God why she was there, then stood up and headed toward the door. She walked past the dining room, and as she pushed the front door open, somebody called, "Mrs. McCain!"

She turned, and there in the dining room stood two dozen tired-looking young men. She recognized several of the players who were on crutches or in slings from injuries—guys she had been sending notes and praying for. Others were redshirt freshmen who had just finished one of Coach Yox's grueling two-hour 5:30 a.m. Saturday workouts. They all looked like she felt. Worn out. Beaten.

"What are you doing here?" Aairon asked.

Laurie swallowed and took a short breath before explaining that she had come for a meeting but the other people couldn't make it. She was heading outside to wait for Tiger Walk.

"Why don't you stay and talk to us," the players said. "Tiger Walk doesn't start for over an hour."

Why not? she thought. So Laurie stayed, and they sat around a table and talked about injuries and workouts and how hard Yox pushed them and what it felt like not to be on the bus with the team. There were moments of optimism. Every player knew he would be on the bus soon. The injured had been there and would return. The redshirts knew their days were coming.

For an amazing few minutes, Laurie and the players became

wounded healers for one another, each reaching out of their pain to help the other and finding comfort in the process. The players did not know exactly what Laurie was experiencing, but they knew her son was hurting. At the same time, Laurie saw what every young man on the team looked like when he wasn't succeeding on the field. She thought she had come to Sewell Hall to meet with the other mothers; instead, she realized she was there to sit and pray with these players. She walked out knowing what she had to do. On Monday she drove to a gift shop and bought boxes and boxes of note cards. More cards. More cookies. More notes. More prayers.

The next home game was three weeks later against Ole Miss, and Laurie's prayer for a companion in her new ministry was answered that afternoon when she looked up to see Teresa Caudle, mother of quarterback Neil Caudle, standing at the door of Sewell Hall. Laurie and Teresa would pray together before each of the final three home games, and Teresa would join Laurie's card and cookie ministry.

SON OF A DEPORTEE

JANUARY 2008

I N FOURTEEN YEARS as chaplain, I have stood with players through injury, illness, and the deaths of parents and siblings. Until 2007 I had never seen a player's father deported from the United States.

Twenty years before Mike Blanc was born, his parents sought hope where others saw only despair. Moname and Mary Blanc lived in Haiti, where president-for-life François Duvalier made sure that anyone who opposed him was killed. Thirty thousand people were murdered. Haitian society barely functioned, and in many areas, it had become a hellhole. Dark paganism was the accepted religion, and children were routinely sold into prostitution or debt-slavery by their starving parents.

Moname and Mary were barely twenty years old, and they knew their only hope lay across the water. There was no future in Haiti for them or any children they might have. They had heard about boats leaving the northwestern shore for the United States, but the price of passage was more than a thousand dollars. Even if they came up with the money, there was no guarantee they would arrive in Miami alive. That didn't matter. They had to go.

Mike speaks softly when he tells the little bit he knows about his parents' voyage. He is a three-hundred-pound defensive lineman who normally radiates light from his bright eyes and quick smile. He laughs easily, and when he speaks, his Haitian accent is thick with the Caribbean. But he speaks softly when he tells me, "They didn't have a motor. The boat was almost like a big raft with a sail. A lot of people were crowded on, and some people got sick with a lot of diseases, and some people died. It was very rough."

Moname and Mary survived the voyage and waded ashore at Miami. In those days legal status wasn't as hard to acquire as today, and they found their way to a neighborhood of Haitian immigrants. Then they found minimum-wage jobs and immediately began sending money back to relatives. "When you're a family from Haiti and you make it to the United States," Mike says, "it's your duty to take care of the ones left behind. You send help, because if you live in Haiti and you don't have somebody sending you money or clothing, you're not going to get it from anywhere else."

Mike was born twenty years after his parents arrived in

the United States, the youngest of five children. He was three years old when his parents divorced. "I didn't realize until later that my oldest brother didn't have a childhood," he says. "He wanted to play football and run track, but by middle school he was driving our mom to work and picking her up, because she never learned to drive or speak English very well. After school he took her to the grocery store and ran errands. He couldn't play sports. He had to grow up fast."

At least once a month, Mike's mother sent money and clothes to cousins in Haiti, and every two or three years she saved enough money to go there herself. When Mike was older, she said, she would take him to her homeplace.

As a young teenager, Mike walked the neighborhood streets after supper, and he was making the kind of choices that would lead to trouble. Then he started looking into the eyes of the men hanging out, and Mike says, "It was real negative." Some of those men said to him, "Man, I wish I were your age. I wish I could go back and do it over again. I'd do it all different." He heard it so many times, Mike decided never to become one of those men. He would escape.

Football gave Mike his best hope. He arrived at Auburn in 2006 and stepped into an unexpected legacy among the defensive linemen. In my earliest years as chaplain, d-linemen like Spencer Johnson, Dexter Murphy, and Reggie Torbor supported everything we were trying to do with the Fellowship of Christian Athletes ministry. Those guys later mentored the younger players coming in, like Quentin Groves and Antonio

Coleman, who then became leaders for Mike Blanc, Antoine Carter, and others. They're like generations, fathers to sons, the older players guiding the younger ones.

These are the kind of young men Jesus surrounded Himself with: impulsive, rough, bold. Antoine Carter came to Auburn with a reputation and a tattoo under his eyes: HOT BOY. Antonio Coleman took Hot under his wing and helped him grow into a respected leader on the defense. Hot later told a reporter that he had thought about having the tattoo removed, explaining, "I think I'm going to keep it, because every time I look in the mirror, it reminds me how far I've come. It's kind of like motivation." That was the influence Mike Blanc fell under.

· · ·

One morning a few weeks after the 2007 season ended, Mike stood in the doorway to my office, and he was not smiling. His mother had called to tell him that his father had been deported to Haiti. She didn't tell him why, but there must have been some trouble. It didn't make sense to Mike. His parents had been in the United States for twenty years longer than Mike had been alive. For the next several days Mike wondered where his father was and what he was doing. He came to my office and sat on the sofa, holding onto his phone and praying that it would ring. Finally his father called, and he sounded lifeless— like a man trying to make the best of a prison sentence. "I'm just thankful to be alive," he told Mike. "Thankful to be breathing and looking at the sun. Thankful to have my health."

Mike was not convinced. After all those years in the United

States, his father was in Port-au-Prince with no job and no hope for one, living with an aunt. There are plenty of miserable places in the world, but few are more miserable, more hopeless than Haiti. Look at a map of the island of Hispaniola, and you'll see the Dominican Republic to the east, dark green and heavily forested. Haiti, to the west, is brown. Almost all of the trees have been cut down to make charcoal, and every storm that crosses the country washes massive mudslides. Moname Blanc had escaped from this place in the 1970s. Now he was back. Mike wanted to help his father, but all he could do was talk to him on the phone.

Then Mike said to his father, "Here, talk to Brother Chette," and he handed the phone to me.

What hope could I give? What comfort? None immediately. I couldn't find a job or food or a home for him. So I talked to him about his son. I told him how much Mike had grown in the short time I had known him. From the first day he arrived on campus, Mike had come to almost every Bible study and FCA meeting. Some players come eager to grow spiritually but then cool off over time. Not Mike. He recruited more guys to come with him. On the field, Mike was working his way into a starting position in 2008. Like so many of our players, I thought of Mike like a son. He even wore jersey number 93, the same number my older brother Quency had worn at Auburn, and that strengthened our bond.

As we ended our conversation I told Moname that he could be very proud of his son. He was on his way. Then I prayed for the Holy Spirit to bring him comfort. It was the best I had to offer.

Blessed are those who mourn, for they will be comforted.

MATTHEW 5:4

DOWN THE SINK

AUGUST 2008

THREE WEEKS BEFORE the first game of the 2008 season, Aairon Savage stood in front of his locker and pulled his shoulder pads and jersey on like it was the first time. Finally, he felt no pain in his shoulder. He walked out of the locker room toward the practice field with no pain in his ankle. Not even a twinge. It was a brand-new day. The first day of practice in pads. He could go full speed again. Full speed for the first time in two years.

He stepped into the sun, and he didn't care how hot it was (ninety-three degrees). He just wanted to play, to put behind him the injuries that had kept him on the sidelines for so much of his sophomore season: South Florida, Vanderbilt, Arkansas, LSU, Ole Miss, Clemson. Aairon had missed them all with shoulder and ankle injuries.

I followed the players out the back door of the air-conditioned Athletic Complex and stepped into the east Alabama August heat, and we walked to the intramural fields. That's where Coach Tuberville always started preseason practice.

I watched Aairon for a while, and he was playing his safety position faster and stronger than ever, flying all over the field. When the team broke for water, he had already intercepted two passes—just the kind of start he needed. After the break, the defensive backs set up in man-to-man coverage, and on the second play, Kodi Burns threw toward Aairon's receiver. Aairon turned to play the ball and jumped high. When he came down awkwardly on his right leg, he screamed, and everyone who heard the scream shuddered.

There's always pain on a football field. You hear the sound of it on almost every play. Bodies crashing against bodies. Helmets cracking helmets. Grunts and groans on every collision. Then sometimes you hear the cry that pierces through all the others—a cry of fear as much as pain—because the player knows in that instant the game might be taken away for him forever. Every player who hears the cry is thankful it isn't him.

Zac Etheridge heard Aairon from across the field. "When it first happened," he says, "the way he fell, you thought it was an ankle. Then to hear him holler. You think about your teammate, your friend, and you pray for him. Knowing Aairon and knowing how hard he likes to compete—to see a guy who works that hard every day in workout, to see him lying on the ground and to hear him holler out. It was tough."

Aairon remembers thinking, *This is it. All my dreams are going down the sink.*

The medical staff hurried onto the field and stabilized Aairon's knee, then put him on a stretcher.

Aairon had dislocated his right kneecap and torn both the anterior cruciate (ACL) and medial collateral (MCL) ligaments. He spent two days in a hospital in Birmingham as his doctors made sure blood was flowing properly to his knee. "I was at the bottom of the world," Aairon says. "I wasn't even sure I would walk again, much less play football."

Our first game was three weeks away, but for Aairon the season was over before it started. He could only look ahead to 2009, the first time he might hope to be back on the field in a game. The road ahead of him was the definition of drudgery. Days and days of rehabilitation on his knee, and as soon as his doctor cleared him, he would be back into the weight room, working on his upper body and his good leg, often while his teammates were outside practicing.

Although nobody could do the work for him, Aairon says he never felt completely alone. "The injury and that time was a pivotal moment in my walk with Christ," he says. "Before that, I would go to church here and there. Say a prayer. It was more like a routine. After my injury, I had support from everywhere, especially my mom and my aunt. They're really deep in the Bible. Always on the phone praying with me and quoting Bible verses. I started building from there."

That summer other mothers were also praying for Aairon.

Several Birmingham-area moms joined Laurie McCain and Teresa Caudle: Donna Hawthorne (Tim's mom), Lynn Trotter (Barrett's mom), and Lisa Christopher (Wade's mom). They met regularly through the summer at Laurie's house to pray for specific players and coaches and to visit and support each other. Andrew McCain was letting Laurie know who needed their prayer support, and they left each meeting with the names of the players they would be sending cards and cookies to the next week.

Laurie had invited Sandra Pugh, who lived nearby in Hoover, several times to join the group at her house, but Sandra couldn't get past the discomfort of Ryan having taking Andrew's starting spot. Then Ryan told Andrew that his mother had been diagnosed with breast cancer—it's not just the injured players who think their life is going down the sink—Andrew called Laurie, and the mothers started praying for Sandra.

"Laurie wouldn't stop reaching out to me," Sandra says, "but I had one excuse or another to not participate in the prayer meetings. When I wound up with breast cancer, she sent me an email offering to put me on the prayer list and inviting me to prayer meeting. I thought, *I'm going to go. I need to be around other mothers, especially if they're willing to pray for me.*"

What Sandra might not have known was that the mothers weren't the only ones praying for her. Their sons had put her name right beside Aairon's on the prayer list and were lifting her up at our summer Bible study and during our Friday night prayers, asking God not to let anybody's dreams slip away.

SOPHOMORE
STRUGGLES

FALL 2008

ONE PLAYER'S MOM calls 2008 "the year everything fell apart."

It wasn't supposed to be that way. After the terrible start in 2007, we had won eight of our last ten games. Then we ended the season on an incredible high note when Kodi Burns scored a touchdown in overtime to beat Clemson in the Chick-fil-A Bowl. Our new offensive coordinator had brought a spread offense system that was suited to Kodi's speed. And the freshmen who had played a huge role in winning those final eight games were bigger, faster, and stronger sophomores after spending the spring and summer with Coach Yox.

But Kodi wasn't locked in as the starter. Neil Caudle, who

was a year older than Kodi, could have played quarterback for plenty of college football teams. As a high school senior, one recruiting service ranked him the seventh-best pro-style quarterback in the country, ahead of Sam Bradford, Christian Ponder, and Andy Dalton, all future NFL starters. When our coaches introduced the spread offense, Neil adapted his style, and in the spring he competed for the starting spot. Then Chris Todd, who had run the spread in high school and at Texas Tech, transferred to Auburn, and Neil fell to third on the depth chart, behind Chris and Kodi.

That might have been Neil's cue to leave.

"Some people believe quarterbacks are made to transfer," Neil says. "I don't buy into that. I made a commitment to Auburn, and I've never given up on anything."

The season started without a clear decision on the starting quarterback. Kodi started the first game, with Chris alternating. Then Chris started against Southern Miss. Kodi threw an interception in the third quarter of that game, and that was the end of the day for him. After the game Coach Tuberville announced that Chris would be the starter the next week.

For nineteen-year-old Kodi, those were tough words.

This may be the part I hate most about college football, and it's the reason I'm a chaplain and not a coach. Only one guy can play quarterback, and the coach has to decide who that guy is, no matter how much he likes all the rest. The kids just have to deal with it.

A great athlete and a great young man like Kodi, who had

experienced the intoxicating cheers of a stadium filled with people calling his name, was benched, and he was deeply hurt. For a while he stopped going to class. He didn't want to be around the other players. His parents were twelve hours away in Arkansas, so he couldn't go home. He could only talk to them on the phone.

Even years later, reflecting on those painful days, Kodi doesn't say much. "I was torn up and broken," he says. "It was a hard transition for me, but during that time I did a lot of growing up. I learned that I couldn't handle everything on my own. I have to trust in God."

Kodi wasn't the only player struggling in his sophomore season. After his successful freshman year, kicker Wes Byrum started the 2008 season with a missed field goal in the opening game, which was a blowout, so no harm done. Then he missed two more kicks against Mississippi State, a game we barely won, 3–2, and for the first time ever he began to question himself. He changed his technique, looking for answers and beating himself up. Kicking had always come naturally to Wes, and suddenly it was slipping away, along with his confidence. Instead of focusing on his spot, he thought about his steps and his right foot. Then he missed an extra point against Vanderbilt, and we lost 14–13.

We lost the next three games to Arkansas, West Virginia, and Ole Miss, and Wes remembers the people who had been slapping him on the back a year earlier were asking him why he wasn't out practicing more. Everybody had an answer.

Wes turned to Al Del Greco, a man who had traveled the same road Wes was traveling now.

Al was my teammate in the early 1980s and one of the best kickers in Auburn history. In his final game, he made three field goals, the last one with twenty-three seconds left in the game to beat Michigan 9–7 in the Sugar Bowl, giving us a chance at a national championship.

A year earlier, however, Al had started his junior season badly, missing four of his first five field goal attempts. He had lost his focus, and whatever he tried, he couldn't get his mind right. It was a lonely time for him. Al believed that if he didn't straighten up, Coach Pat Dye would bench him.

"Let's face it," he says, "kicking is 85 percent mental. It's a state of mind. A confidence level. Borderline cockiness.

"Every player goes onto the field wanting to be flawless on every play. Even if you're not, your teammates can still make that play a success. Or if other players mess up, they can line up on the next play and do better. But if a kicker misses a field goal, the play fails every time. He might have to wait a quarter or longer to get back onto the field. And if he misses a kick at the end of the game, he has to live with that all week before he has a chance to make it up. And each miss weighs you down more."

Wes talked with Al several times during the season, and each time Al reminded him to trust his leg and his technique. Forget the mistakes, and put those things behind. Focus on the goal and think on *good* things. Have faith.

"That kick you made at Florida as a freshman," Al reminded

him. "To make that again after Urban Meyer called time-out—that was an unbelievable accomplishment. In your whole career you might not face a situation as important and as physically and mentally taxing as that one. You've conquered it. You've done it. Now you just need to make a few easy ones and get it going again."

But Morgan Hull took over the kickoff duties halfway through the 37–20 homecoming win. The next week Wes missed a 42-yard field goal attempt against Georgia, and his season was over. His right knee was inflamed. When we scored a touchdown later in the game, Morgan was sent in to kick the extra point.

STORMS RISING

OUR FEAR . . . GOD'S PEACE

O N FRIDAY, NOVEMBER 21, 2008, the Auburn campus was clearing out fast as students hit the road home for Thanksgiving week. It was one of those peaceful days on campus when you feel like you have the whole place to yourself. We had an open date the next day (the Alabama game was eight days later, on November 29), so practice was just a session of walk-throughs. When we finished, most of the players drove home to their families or went to their friends' families for the weekend.

That same day, three hundred miles away, the backup quarterback for the University of Florida heard a knock at his door.

His long, difficult journey was about to begin.

. . .

Eight days later Alabama was beating us badly in the final game of the season, and up in the stands at Bryant-Denny Stadium, Laurie McCain literally bumped into Dawn Ziemba in the aisle. Laurie tried to recover with a sweet comment—she had never been completely comfortable with Dawn since her son Lee had taken Andrew's starting job a year earlier—and she stumbled over her words.

Dawn, like most of the Auburn parents that day, wasn't in the mood for sweetness. They were watching their sons fall further and further behind, and they were angry. The season had turned sour on the road in Nashville, with the 14–13 loss to Vanderbilt. Four days later our offensive coordinator had been dismissed, and we won only one of the next five games. Now we were trailing Alabama 29–0, and it was getting worse.

Lee had played the entire season at offensive tackle with a torn lateral meniscus, putting off surgery until December. The whole thing felt like a waste to Dawn, and she didn't mask her frustration.

Laurie was a little put off—at least Dawn's son was playing—and she decided there wasn't much she could say that would help. Jesus told us to love everybody, but sometimes it's best to walk away and put some distance between yourself and people you might find hard to love.

. . .

I've seen December storms before at Auburn, but nothing like the one in 2008. The Athletic Complex, with its dark gray concrete interior walls, felt like a bunker in the days following the disappointing season and the 36–0 loss to Alabama. Telephones were ringing, and rumors about the future of the coaching staff came from every direction, even from the local elementary schools, where the coaches' children heard them.

On the first Tuesday morning in December, the coaches gathered for their weekly staff meeting,

For ten years Tommy Tuberville had begun every Tuesday morning staff meeting by asking me to lead a Bible study. Week after week we came together to hear God's Word, and then we did our best to put those words into practice, to build our foundation on a rock. Now the storm was upon us. We knew that later in the day Tommy would be sitting down with athletic director Jay Jacobs to discuss Tommy's tenure at Auburn. The day before, Tommy had met with the university president, Jay Gogue. The future of the entire staff was in question. Although I am not a member of the coaching staff— I am employed by the Fellowship of Christian Athletes—my role as chaplain was also in jeopardy. Tommy had invited me to Auburn when he was hired in 1999. If he left or was replaced, the new coach might want to bring in his own chaplain or not want a chaplain at all.

Tommy stepped away from the head of the table, as he did every week, and I stood at his place and turned to the scripture I had used five years earlier, another stormy time. In Mark 6 the apostles are in a boat crossing the Sea of Galilee, straining against a headwind that had swirled into a full-blown storm. I looked down that long conference table with coaches on each side, none of us knowing where we might be by week's end, and I realized we too were in a boat in the dark, straining our eyes to see the stars to navigate by, while waves pounded against us.

At the darkest moment the disciples looked across the water and saw a ghost coming toward them, and they cried out, terrified.

I was reading the story to the coaches, but I needed to hear the words too. I'm supposed to be the chaplain, the pastor, the one with so much faith that I never fear. But I'm also a husband and a father of three children, and sometimes in my concern for my family's well-being, I shove Jesus out of the way and grab the oars myself. Then I try to push our little boat through the storm. Suddenly I am alone and afraid. Would a church call me as pastor? Another school? Ten years earlier God called me to Auburn, and I hadn't heard Him call me anywhere else. Where would we go?

The disciples saw no ghost, of course. It was Jesus, who cried out to His friends, "Take courage! It is I. Don't be afraid."

I read Jesus' words aloud to the coaches, then I read them again and listened to them myself. "Take courage!"

I continued reading: "Then He climbed into the boat with them, and the wind died down."

The lesson for us was clear: when we try to row through the storms alone, even with the help of our family and friends, the waves and wind are too much for us. Only when we let Jesus into the boat with us does the wind die down.

The words sounded so simple, yet in the midst of the storm they can be hard to trust. We want God to take action. To do something. We need a miracle we can see.

God doesn't promise miracles. He promises peace. He promises comfort. In the most familiar chapter of the Bible, the Twenty-third Psalm, the path leads the psalmist into the valley of the shadow of death, the place we fear most.

But even in the midst of our most difficult trials, we know, "you are with me; your rod and your staff, they comfort me."

The coaches and I prayed together around the conference table as we had prayed hundreds of times before for family members and friends, for strength in our marriages, for players dealing with injuries or facing other difficult trials. We asked Jesus to step back into the boat with us, to calm the storms of our hearts and allow us to experience His peace.

In that moment, He was there. In our prayer we turned toward His face and away from our own uncertainty, and I could feel the tension easing in my spine and my neck muscles relaxing. Jesus would not remove this storm, but He would ride it out with us. He would give us strength, peace, and courage for the journey.

• • •

Laurie McCain experienced what she calls her "foot-washing moment," one she is not proud of. It came quickly.

Andrew had asked her to check on Lee Ziemba, who was in Birmingham for surgery to repair his meniscus, on Tuesday morning while we were in our Bible study. Laurie knew she should go visit and support his family, just as she had visited other players for two seasons. But the encounter with Dawn at the Alabama game had been so uncomfortable, she really didn't want to see her again. Then she thought about the surgical facility, with only chips and drinks in the vending machines, and she knew they would need food. So she packed some sandwiches and cookies and drove to the hospital, hoping she might slip in and out quickly.

She went to the waiting area and sighed, relieved, when she didn't see the Ziembas. Lee must have already gone into surgery. She asked at the nurses' station if they would take the sandwiches up to the family.

"Why? You know where to go," the nurse said.

She was right. Laurie had gone up dozens of times to deliver food and to visit players and their families. So she walked slowly to the elevator and rode up. The door opened, and there stood Dawn. Laurie was so nervous, she just started talking. "I'm so sorry for what has happened. Here's some food. We feel so bad for Lee. Andrew thinks the world of him." She kept talking, not giving Dawn a chance to say anything, until finally Dawn just started crying.

In the turmoil of rumors and meetings, nobody from Auburn had checked on Lee. "Of all the people who should have cared about us," she told Laurie, "it was you that came."

Then Laurie started crying and admitted she had been afraid to come, believing Dawn wouldn't want to see her. "What can I do for you?" Laurie asked. "Can I bring anything? Pray for Lee or for you?"

"I'm sure Lee wants you to pray for him," Dawn said.

In an instant a friendship was born, and there was peace.

. . .

That night in Auburn, Angie and Jay Jacobs had invited my wife, Lakeba, and me to their home for an event to support a camp their daughter and ours had attended the previous summer. The group was small, maybe eight or ten people, and I noticed Angie had to carry much of the conversation. Jay, who is usually relaxed and engaged, appeared occupied with his thoughts. When the last of the guests were leaving, I asked him, "You okay?"

He hesitated a moment and replied, "No, I'm not. Can you stay a little longer?"

"Sure," I said.

He asked me to join him in his study, so I followed him in and waited for him to speak. I wondered if his concern had something to do with the discussions with Tommy.

In that silent moment I considered my own awkward position. Two of my closest friends were engaged in tense negotiations that had a direct impact on my family and me. Both of them had their own pastors, and yet my relationship with each of them was in many ways pastoral. Jay and I call each other *Paraclete*, a Greek word that means "one who consoles or comforts, who encourages or uplifts." That is what Jay is to me—my encourager. He tells me that is my role in his life. And Tommy made our FCA ministry possible by envisioning the position of a full-time chaplain for the football players. He selected me to build the ministry and to lead it. For ten years he had supported us in every way. Earlier that day I had prayed with Tommy in the minutes before he went into Jay's office. Now I was alone with Jay in his study.

"Chette," Jay said finally, "I think there's a storm coming."

The entire world seemed to be talking about his meeting with Tommy. Newspapers had reported it, and sports radio had speculated about the outcome all afternoon. What they didn't know was that Jay had begun the conversation Tuesday believing Tommy would continue as head coach. By the end of the discussion, Jay had heard enough to believe Tommy might resign on Wednesday.

I decided to tell him about the coaches Bible study that morning—about the storm and the importance of keeping Jesus in the boat—and the peace I had experienced when I called on Him. Jay suggested that we pray together, and as we did, we asked Jesus to come back into his boat. I looked for signs of peace in Jay, but his demeanor did not change. He simply thanked me, and we said good night.

Only later did Jay tell me the rest of the story.

When I arrived at Jay's house that night, he was processing in his mind the steps he would take if Tommy resigned. "The only other major hiring experience I had," he said later, "was the baseball coach. Certainly, God was able to use that experience to help equip me some to hire the head football coach, but I knew this would be a completely different deal."

As Jay and I prayed together in his study for direction and peace, the memory of a conversation from nearly four years earlier came back to him. In January 2005, three weeks after Jay had been named athletic director, the University of Texas hired our defensive coordinator, Gene Chizik, to be assistant head coach.

We all hated to see Gene leave. Like the other coaches, Lakeba and I had become close friends with Gene and his wife, Jonna, during their three years at Auburn. We were young in our marriages, and our children were about the same age, so we had much in common. We were passionate and growing in our faith, and when I started a second coaches Bible study, in addition to the one at the weekly staff meetings, Gene and Eddie Gran, our running backs coach, were the first to join. They invited others, and the fellowship grew. But the nature of the business is that coaches move on to take advantage of greater opportunities, and the Texas job was the next step on the road to a head coach position for Gene.

Before leaving Auburn, Gene asked Jay for a few minutes of his time. The moment was brief, but the two men connected at a deeper, spiritual level.

Neither Jay nor Gene suggested anything about Gene ever coming back to Auburn. That thought wasn't on either man's horizon. Auburn had just finished the season undefeated, and Gene was headed in another direction. But watching Gene leave his office, Jay felt God putting on his heart, "Gene Chizik is one of My guys. This is a man I trust—a faithful man."

Suddenly, four years later, in the midst of our prayer in Jay's study, Jay thought of Gene, and he began to see a potential scenario lining up if Tommy resigned. Gene Chizik might be a candidate. As defensive coordinator at Auburn in 2004 and Texas in 2005, he had helped lead consecutive teams to undefeated seasons and had been one of the most respected assistant coaches in the country.

In that moment, Jay says today, "I felt a peacefulness that is unexplainable. Don't misunderstand me. It wasn't peaceful every moment. But my heart was at peace when I gave in to the Holy Spirit. When I kept Jesus in the boat. Along the way I occasionally set Him off to the side when the waves got really rough, and I tried to row myself. But He always got back in with me."

On Wednesday, Tommy resigned, and the storm intensified when the news was announced. Many words were spoken and written, some cruel and mean-spirited, regarding Jay, Tommy, and Tommy's assistants and their families. Some relationships did not survive the pounding. But God blessed me with the opportunity to pray with all of them, to cry with them, and to witness the Holy Spirit reassuring them—granting them (and me) peace and comfort through the stormy days and nights.

At home, Lakeba and I saw and experienced for ourselves the truth of Hebrews 13:5: "Never will I leave you; never will I forsake you."

Jay began the search process for a new head football coach by asking God's guidance every day. He believed God had put Gene Chizik on his heart and mind for a reason. He also knew he had to test that belief. "Sometimes intuition is just that," he says. "It's of the flesh. But if I'm in the right spot spiritually in my walk with God, it can actually be the power of the Holy Spirit at work in my own life. I'm learning how to hear the Holy Spirit speak to me, and what I'm learning is that the more I will sit and listen, the louder His voice is."

Jay also knows that his job is to hire coaches who will win, and in two years as a head coach at Iowa State, Gene had a 5–19 record and a ten-game losing streak. Jay stepped back and looked at Gene's entire body of work, listening to both his heart and his head.

"It wasn't a logical move," Jay says. But he was reminded of Proverbs 29:26 ("Many seek an audience with a ruler, but it is from the LORD that man gets justice"), the verse he quoted the day he became athletic director, and his commitment to listen to and serve God first. God's ways often defy logic.

FAITH, PERSISTENCE, AND VISION

ONE OF MY favorite broken road stories is about Bartimaeus, the blind man who sat and begged by the side of the road at the gate of Jericho. In Bible times the city gate was where you found out what was going on—who's doing this or that, who's spending time with whom—like standing on the corner back home.

Bartimaeus learned that Jesus was coming, and he figured this was his chance for a miracle. To see! When he heard a big crowd coming, he knew that such crowds always surrounded Jesus, and he cried out, "Jesus, Son of David, have mercy on me!"

Immediately, the people standing nearest to Jesus rebuked Bartimaeus and told him to be quiet, but he didn't listen to them. Instead, he cried out all the more.

I love the blind man's persistence. Jesus didn't respond the first time Bartimaeus called, so he called again. He would not be intimidated by the crowd or denied his opportunity to come face-to-face with Christ. He had lived his life in darkness, and the Healer was coming his way, so he was willing to make a scene if he had to, right there at the city gate.

Jesus heard Bartimaeus and said to the people, "Call him."

Then He asked the blind man the same question He asks us every day: "What do you want me to do for you?"

Common sense, at this point, should have told Bartimaeus that this man couldn't help. He'd heard promises all his life from healers and conjurers, and he still couldn't see. Plus Jesus was a popular and important man. Why would He help a poor, blind beggar?

But Bartimaeus acted on faith, believing Jesus was the light of the world, and he asked for the impossible. "Rabbi," he said, "I want to see."

Every time I read that question and answer, Bartimaeus challenges me to ask Christ for the impossible. Not to settle for what common sense tells me are the limits of His possibilities.

"Go," Jesus told Bartimaeus, "your faith has healed you." And immediately the blind man could see.

Now see what Bartimaeus did with his gift. He followed Jesus up the road to Jerusalem and the triumphal entry, which we remember as Palm Sunday. I believe Christ gave this man vision so he could see mighty acts, just as I believe He lets each of us witness His mighty acts when we follow Him in faith.

CHOOSING

DECEMBER 2008

J AY INTERVIEWED SEVERAL successful head coaches who had support among Auburn people. Whoever he chose, our football program would succeed. Then he told me he was considering Gene Chizik, and I felt the moment I heard his name, Gene was the right man. I couldn't have told you how many wins or losses Gene had as a head coach, although I knew the record wasn't good. When word leaked that Jay was considering Gene Chizik, almost nobody cheered. Some even booed. Gene had been an extremely successful defensive coordinator with two consecutive undefeated seasons. But his two years as head coach at Iowa State had changed everything in the minds of many fans.

Jay faced a situation where common sense and faith directly opposed each other. The safe thing for him would have been to hire an established head coach with a winning record. But he was not convinced the safe way was the right way. He asked me to pray with him, and in his office, with its huge windows looking out at Jordan-Hare Stadium, Beard-Eaves Memorial Coliseum, and Plainsman Park, we went down on our knees and asked God to give Jay clarity.

Much was at stake for the university—and for the Jacobs family. "There was no doubt in my mind or my wife's mind," Jay says, "that if this did not work out, it meant that we would not be here."

But Jay arose with conviction. He told President Gogue that Gene Chizik was the man. He did not explain his method for arriving at that decision, nor did Dr. Gogue ask. "A more detailed explanation for hiring Gene certainly would have been warranted," Jay says, "but he did not ask. That's what you want—to be responsible for your own actions and decisions. And though the decision didn't make logical sense, I was as at peace with it as you can possibly be."

On December 13, Gene Chizik was introduced as Auburn's new head football coach.

UNITY

I N HIS FIRST MEETING with the players, Coach Chizik assured them that he wasn't looking to rebuild. His plan was to win now. His last season as Auburn's defensive coordinator in 2004 had ended 13–0, and he expected to be right back there.

Success requires unity, and Gene and his staff faced the prospect of a divided locker room the first day they stepped onto campus. The previous season Chris Todd had started five of the first six games at quarterback. After the offensive coordinator was replaced, Kodi Burns started the last six games. A lot of the players had their favorites, and nothing divides a locker room like a quarterback controversy.

Pride lies at the root of every divided locker room.

A player believes he deserves more playing time. A receiver and a running back think they should get more touches. A special player appears to be receiving special treatment. Offense believes defense isn't pulling its share of the load, or vice versa. Players start grumbling about coaches and then about other players. The new staff couldn't afford any of that, and yet they could only ask the players to trust them. They could not select the starting quarterback until they had seen Kodi and Chris with their own eyes. But Chris was recovering from off-season shoulder surgery, so he couldn't show his best during spring practice. Coaches had to wait until fall practice to see both quarterbacks on the practice field.

On August 13, three weeks before the first game, Kodi stood in my doorway. I knew in an instant that the coaches had selected Chris as the starter. Two years after arriving at Auburn as a five-star, running-passing, rising superstar, Kodi's future had unfolded into something he didn't recognize. Not only had Chris been named starting quarterback, they had asked Kodi to change positions and become a wide receiver—to give up the dream of ever playing quarterback at Auburn again.

I grow so close to these players, it pains me to see them broken by a game they love so much.

Kodi and I spent a long time talking and praying, and though I don't remember the words either of us spoke, I knew when he left my office that he would stand strong as a positive influence in the locker room despite the pain he was experiencing. Soon I would see how powerful an impact he would become.

Later that day, at a team meeting, Coach Chizik announced that Chris would be the starting quarterback. Kodi asked to speak to his teammates, and over the next few minutes he spoke more powerfully than any sermon I will ever preach. Nobody in that room will ever forget what Kodi said and demonstrated that day. He didn't try to hide his pain. He told us how badly it hurt to be passed over. But he reminded his teammates that they were a family. He would support Chris and the coaches' choice, and he would not allow the decision to divide the locker room.

I am convinced that Kodi's talk was Auburn's first step on the road to the national championship seventeen months later. His sacrifice inspired and challenged others to commit even more. Over the next two seasons, Kodi lived out his promise. He had many key moments in big games, including scoring the first touchdown in the national championship game. None of those plays, however, was more important or more memorable than his words to his teammates on August 13, 2009.

RUNNING BY FAITH

SEPTEMBER 2009

Gus MALZAHN, OUR offensive coordinator, wanted speed. Go! Go! Go! His hurry-up, no-huddle offense was designed to run like a two-minute drill for the entire game. Snap the ball less than five seconds after the referee spots it, and the defense won't have time to substitute or adjust. Do that long enough, and you wear down the defenders. Of course, our offense had to be in top physical condition for it to work.

In the days leading up to the first game of the 2009 season, Gus was never completely satisfied with the speed of the offense in practice. They were running plays faster than they had in their football lives, and Gus wanted more.

If you've ever watched an up-tempo basketball game, when a team rebounds and races down the court play after play until their opponents are dragging themselves down to play defense, then you understand the pace Gus was seeking. The players thought they got it, they said they got it, and yet Gus wanted faster. "That's not good enough," he said. "That's not good enough." The players walked off at the end of practice wondering how much faster they could go, how much more they could give.

Then we won our first game of the season 37–13, and in the second half you could see the impact of the hurry-up, no-huddle. We scored four times and literally wore out the Louisiana Tech defense. Our guys' conditioning and their speed work at practice had turned into touchdown after touchdown.

The next week at practice the offense worked faster than ever during their pace period. What the players earlier believed, they now knew through experience. They saw it work. Gus didn't have to convince them to pick up the pace. They were flying around the field and back to the line of scrimmage again and again.

Tim Jackson, executive associate athletic director, was at every practice and traveled with the team. Tim was also a worship leader at his church, and on Friday night before the Mississippi State game, I asked him to bring his guitar to our chapel service and sing. He chose "Walk by Faith," which includes the lines, "I will walk by faith even when I cannot see well, because this broken road prepares Your will for me." Then he told the players how proud he was that they had faith in Coach Malzahn. They believed in his system even when they could not see the outcome. They had worked harder on conditioning than any other time in their lives, with nothing but a promise of a payoff. Then, on Saturday, they saw the other team wearing down on defense in the third quarter, and *boom, boom, boom,* we were scoring and scoring and scoring.

GET UP,
GET GOING

OCTOBER 24, 2009

AFTER STARTING THE 2009 season with five straight wins, we lost on the road to Arkansas and then at home to Kentucky in a game we thought we should have won. Then on a Saturday night on the road in Baton Rouge, Louisiana, nothing was working for us, and the LSU game got out of hand in a hurry. Fumbles, penalties, an interception, stopped on fourth and inches—and that was just on offense. We trailed 17–0 at halftime, and LSU scored two more touchdowns in the third quarter.

Failure can lead to despair if you do not address it quickly.

Ryan Pugh and Lee Ziemba remember how the coaches responded. "Coach Malzahn was in the press box the first half,"

Ryan says, "but then he came out of the box and coached on the field, and he coached until the final whistle, even knowing we weren't going to win.

"He never thought about giving up on us. He never took anything for granted, and what he did turned a negative into a positive.

"I learned that night that things in life will not always be great. We won't always be winning, so to speak. And if you give up on it and just try to move on, you won't learn anything from it. If you stick with it, keep on playing your hardest, keep on coaching, you may find that you're better for it when the game is over."

Ziemba remembers a similar message delivered by offensive line coach Jeff Grimes. "We were getting our butts kicked," he says. "When the fourth quarter started, we thought we didn't have a chance to win, and none of us wanted to be out there. Everything was going wrong. We couldn't put the ball in the end zone. We couldn't even convert a third down."

Coach Grimes brought all the offensive linemen together and calmly told them, "Anybody can play hard when you're ahead by twenty-eight. It takes a man to play hard when you're down by twenty-eight. Now go out there and play!"

I'm reminded of the Garden of Gethsemane, when the disciples accompanying Jesus fell asleep instead of praying with Him. Three times Jesus found them sleeping at His moment of greatest need. They had been presented with a great opportunity and had failed miserably. They might have drifted into despair, but Jesus did not allow it. Instead, He simply said, "Get up, let us go."

Put this failure behind you. Don't wallow in despair. We have work ahead of us.

More than the words Coach Grimes spoke, Ziemba remembers his demeanor: "We were all disappointed, and he had every reason to be upset with the way we were playing. To have our coach show us he was in it with us even when everything was going wrong, that was important."

On our final possession of the game, the offense drove fifty-nine yards and scored with three seconds left. Not a victory. Not even a moral victory. But Ziemba and Pugh and their teammates left Tiger Stadium that night knowing their coaches would never give up on them, never turn their backs on them. No matter the score, if there was time on the clock, there was time to "get up and get going"—one more series, one more play, one more opportunity.

TRANSFORMATION
IN THE DESERT

OCTOBER 24, 2009

I F YOU DROVE from Auburn to Baton Rouge, you would be a little over halfway to Brenham, Texas. It's a long, long way to the home of Blinn Junior College.

About the time our guys were running onto the field to play LSU, the Blinn Buccaneers' starting quarterback, Cam Newton, was passing for three touchdowns and running for two more scores in an 84–7 homecoming win.

A performance like that in Baton Rouge or in Auburn would have made Cam the lead story on ESPN's SportsCenter. But when he took off his jersey and walked out of the stadium in Brenham, he was almost never recognized. "People in the store might ask if I played football," Cam says, "and when I told them

I played for the junior college, they'd size me up, like I wasn't good enough to play or I had gotten into trouble."

Cam had indeed gotten into trouble that has been chronicled elsewhere, trouble that led to his leaving the University of Florida after two seasons. Cam's transformation was not instant, but it began instantly. When your mother sees you in the worst trouble of your life, and she looks you in the eye and asks, "What are we going to do now?"—you've got a decision to make. Cam's decision included that long car ride to Brenham. The 2009 season was a broken road in the desert for Cam. In the Bible the desert represents more than vast, dry emptiness. It is a place of change, growth, and preparation. So it was for Cam. He told me that when he was in junior college, he thought he had destroyed his life. His Blinn teammates asked, "How was it at Florida? What was Tebow like? What did Percy Harvin do before games?"

Cam had been with those guys every day for two seasons, training, practicing, and playing. Now they were all a memory. History. No more Gatorade at practice. Not even cold water. One pair of cleats for practice and games. Fewer people in the stands than for his high school games.

Five touchdowns in a game might be enough to satisfy some, but Cam wanted more. He wanted to live a life on and off the field that was worthy of his little brother. Cam was twelve years old when his brother was born, and his coming must have touched something deep inside of Cam. "My little brother has been dear to my heart since he was born," he says. "I love kids.

I just want to make them smile." He also wanted to live a life worthy of the gospel of Christ, and during his season in the desert, he began to picture what that life might look like. On game days his mother often gave him a Proverb or another verse to pray. One morning she gave him James 4:10: "Humble yourselves before the Lord, and he will lift you up."

Cam committed the verse to memory. He had been humbled before the world, and now he was beginning to see what it meant to humble himself before the Lord.

GAME DAY:
LOOK UP!

OCTOBER 31, 2009

I WOKE UP on Halloween morning in 2009 to the sound of blowing rain slapping against the hotel room window. It was Saturday, and we had an 11:21 a.m. kickoff at home against Ole Miss, which meant the pregame meal was scheduled for 7:21. Gene often asked me to pray before the meal, so I was careful not to be late. After the blessing, players lined up by position to get their food.

I waited near the end of the line, watching some of the guys pile their plates with eggs, bacon, sausage, and grits, and others stick to lunch food as if they were playing in the late afternoon or evening. I sat down to eat at a few minutes before eight—the same time a dozen or so moms were coming in from the rain at

Auburn to pray together at Sewell Hall.

The mothers were quieter than usual that morning. Maybe it was the weather or the early hour. They didn't spend a lot of time visiting; they went straight to prayers. Laurie McCain remembers, "There was a strange spirit about everybody that day. We couldn't figure it out. It wasn't about winning or losing. We had lost three straight games after winning five straight. The scoreboard wasn't the most important thing to us. We just sensed that we needed to pray for the protection of our sons."

I finished my breakfast with the team, and Dr. Michael Goodlett and I went to the parking lot to ride back to Auburn. The rain stopped somewhere on the road between Montgomery and Auburn, and then there were clouds and wind that would stay with us all day. We parked behind the Athletic Complex, and I went to the locker room and changed clothes, then walked out through the crowd toward the stadium.

At 9:21 the team buses pulled up to Sewell Hall, and the players and coaches stepped out. Most of the players' families go to the same spot along Tiger Walk every Saturday so their sons can find them easily. "We're all looking for our families," Ryan Pugh says. "It's an exciting time for us—one of the most exciting things you get to do as an Auburn football player—and that five seconds with your family means a lot to us."

On that morning, however, Sandra Pugh was not there to greet Ryan. Neither was Teresa Caudle there for Neil, nor Lynn Trotter for Barrett, Donna Hawthorne for Tim, Laurie McCain for Andrew, Abby Downs for Watson, Lisa Christopher for

Wade, nor Dawn Ziemba for Lee. They and the other moms were still praying in Sewell Hall. Something powerful was happening, something none of them understood, and none would be able to explain. Whatever it was, they couldn't leave until they had prayed through it. They couldn't walk outside until each of them had asked the Holy Spirit to place a hedge of protection around their sons, their sons' teammates, and the Ole Miss players. By the time they finished, Tiger Walk was over. The players had walked into the stadium.

Only the student section in Jordan-Hare Stadium was filled when the team stepped onto the field for the first time. It was ninety minutes before kickoff, and the rest of the stadium was empty. The players, still in the clothes they wore for Tiger Walk, walked or jogged across the grass, looking like a bunch of guys about to choose up sides for a Saturday morning backyard game. In that quiet moment in this place, I experienced the same unexplainable peace I feel whenever I walk through my mother's front door or into the Old Mountaintop Baptist Church where I grew up. This is home. God has met me right here more than at any other place on earth, and I cannot walk on this ground without remembering a time of brokenness when He revealed Himself or a time of celebration when He was here.

Following a tradition that Coach Trooper Taylor brought to Auburn, we called everybody together into a circle for a prayer that I began, and after it went around the circle and everybody had prayed, Trooper ended it and said, "Amen." Then it was time for the players to go back to the locker room and suit up.

When the team came back onto the field in their uniforms to warm up, I took a program from a stack in the locker room and carried it out to a bench on the sideline to read what had been written about the players. I smiled when I saw Antonio Coleman's picture on the cover. A.C. is one of my heroes. Nobody I know faced a tougher road than A.C. His brother took his own life when he was released from prison and found his fiancé had been cheating on him. In an instant, fifteen-year-old Antonio became the father figure to five nieces and nephews. A.C.'s older siblings, who might have been able to help, were all in trouble with the law. His mother was on government assistance, so A.C. became the primary breadwinner, working construction jobs in the summertime.

He accepted a football scholarship to Auburn but drove home to Mobile whenever he could to be with the kids, or his mom sometimes brought them up to Auburn. In the midst of all that, A.C. was an All–SEC defensive lineman and could have left Auburn for the NFL draft after the coaching change, but he stayed. Then for the first seven games he had to wonder if he had made the right decision. He injured his wrist, and the cast the doctor put on him made it almost impossible to grab players to tackle them. But the cast had come off before the LSU game, and A.C. had responded with a sack and two tackles for losses.

I hadn't gotten far into reading the program when Jay Boulware, our special teams coach, came over and asked me to pray with him. We took off our hats and knelt there on the sideline in front of the bench as the stands continued to fill with fans—a very private moment in a very public place. We thanked God for this incredible privilege, for our wives and children, for these players and coaches who were so committed to knowing Him and experiencing His love.

Finally the players finished their warm-ups, and I followed them back to the locker room as the public address announcer asked the fans to turn their attention to the flagpole for the flight of Nova, the eagle.

I've never watched the eagle soar over Jordan-Hare Stadium before a football game. I've only seen videos of the pregame flight—eighty-seven thousand people standing and cheering as he glides and banks over the stands before swooping down and landing on the fifty-yard line. Even visiting fans stand and turn toward the flagpole to watch the majestic bird take off and fly free above them. Every flight is different, because even though the eagle is well trained, only he decides where he's going to fly and when he's going to land. *Sports Illustrated* calls it one of the best traditions in all of college football.

After the eagle lands and his trainers take him to the sideline, the Auburn marching band marches down the field playing, "War Eagle, fly down that field . . . ," and for the next twenty minutes the crowd never sits down, whipping itself into a frenzy with singing, cheering, clapping, and stomping.

In those final moments before kickoff you might think Coach Chizik would be working on the players emotionally the way the band, the cheerleaders, and pregame video excite the fans, but that was not his style. Players had prepared themselves physically and mentally all week at practice and in meetings, so by game day they were confident and loose. There was very little nervousness in the locker room. I stood off to the side as the players talked quietly with position coaches or listened to music.

Some of the guys came to me and asked me to pray with them. I've knelt in that locker room thousands of times, and each time I open my eyes, I feel refreshed and renewed. Ryan Pugh says, "Kneeling in prayer takes my mind off the game and puts my focus on the most important thing in my life. To do that moments before stepping onto field in such a great place as Auburn."

One Saturday, early in the season, I looked up, and Gus Malzahn, our offensive coordinator, asked if I would pray with him. For him and Ted Roof, our defensive coordinator, to humble themselves on their knees in front of the entire team touched me. Every Saturday after that first time, Gus and Ted waited with the players to pray with me.

Gene and I prayed together anywhere and everywhere—before the game, after the game, on Friday night and Saturday morning, on buses, in hotel rooms, in his office, and in the locker room. Those pregame moments, while the crowd cheered in the stadium and we knelt below, reminded me of a pastor who spoke of our posture before the Lord, using as his text Psalm 5:3: "My voice You shall hear in the morning, O Lord; in the morning I will direct it to You, and I will look up."

Every morning, before I begin my day, my entire being should be focused on God—looking up as intently as the crowd in the stadium watches the flight of the eagle or as respectfully as they look up at the flag when they sing the national anthem. I go to the Bible and find the many times when Jesus performed miracles, and He looked up to the Father. Too often during the week I allow the distractions of the day to prevent me from looking up. With players coming in and out of my office, I get wrapped up in the doing of God's work and not being in His presence.

Then on Saturday morning, when you might expect us to be focused on anything *except* God, a group of players' mothers began the day by looking up. Before breakfast, in the locker room, and on the sidelines, we looked up, and many of us felt closer to His presence than at any other time of the week.

My prayer time with Chette is extremely vital in my ability to be an effective football coach for the next day's game. I walk away from those times feeling a renewed sense of strength, peace, and focus. Every prayer meeting we have grows my relationship with Christ, and there is nothing that prepares me more for a game than the reminder that we are playing for something much bigger than a win, and on a much larger stage than Jordan-Hare Stadium.

GENE CHIZIK
HEAD COACH, 2009-12

You never know when your last play is going to be.

ZAC ETHERIDGE

DEFENSIVE BACK

JESUS, HELP ME

OCTOBER 31, 2009

THE LOCKER ROOM doors were opened and the song "All I Do Is Win" blasted in from the speakers in the stadium. The guys buckled their helmets and filed out toward the tunnel to wait for their cue. Then they ran onto the field through the Auburn marching band standing in the shape of the AU logo and playing "War Eagle."

The crowd, as always, exploded in cheers, and the players soaked in the adulation as Ole Miss ran in from the other side. I walked around the edge of the field and over to the sideline, and I saw Aairon Savage standing near the bench. I marveled at his commitment. Aairon was missing his second full season as a player because of an Achilles injury. He had graduated almost a year earlier and might have moved on. Yet here he was, looking stronger than ever from his workouts, and doing everything he could to encourage his teammates.

The game started, and toward the end of the first quarter we had the ball. Up in the stands, I would learn later, Zac Etheridge's mother, Cassandra Kelly, thought she could get to the bathroom and back before we went back on defense. Cassandra almost never left her seat, because she didn't want to risk missing one of Zac's plays on defense. She believes it was God's grace that led her to do so this time.

She stepped out of the ladies room, and in the shuffle of people and shouts echoing off the concrete, she thought she heard her son's name over the public address system. *Oh,* she thought, *Zac must have made a play.* She hurried through the crowd to get to an opening where she could see the field. Just as she got to the top of the aisle, her daughter came running up the steps. Zac was hurt. They had called on the phone from the field and said to come down.

Cassandra looked down to the field and saw the group of men, including Coach Chizik, huddled around what looked like two players down. One of them must have been Zac. She reached out to grab the wall to steady herself before she started down the aisle. Cassandra was a nurse, so she was accustomed to dealing with medical emergencies. But not if the emergency involved her son. Not if they had to call for her to come down to the field. Her daughter took her by the arm, and they walked down.

Cassandra immediately began praying silently: *Oh, Lord, You've got to take care of my boy. You've got to heal him. I'm claiming that right now. Claiming Your healing. I know we're here by Your stripes, but I'm his mother. I'm emotional, and I'm asking You to heal my boy.*

The stadium was deathly quiet, and the silence frightened Cassandra all the more. She couldn't cry out. It was so quiet, everyone in the stadium would hear her. She looked down the aisle for Donald, her husband, and saw him near the bottom of the aisle, looking up toward her. She hurried down, pulling away from her daughter. The security guard standing beside Donald let them step through an opening in a low brick wall and onto the grass, then he led them around the hedge to the sideline, where Jonna Chizik met them.

Cassandra doesn't remember much else, except, "I was hysterical."

Moments earlier, when his mom was in the bathroom, Zac, playing safety, had flown in and jumped over an Ole Miss guard to help make a tackle. At the same time, Antonio Coleman had shaken his blocker, and he dove in from the other direction. Zac and A.C. collided full speed just above the runner, Rodney Scott, and a surge like a lightning bolt exploded down Zac's spine and all the way to his fingertips and toes. Zac heard the whistle blow and tried to pop up after the tackle, but nothing happened. His arms and legs wouldn't move. He couldn't feel them. He blinked to make sure he was conscious. He was. He could see the painted grass just inches from his nose. Zac's face-mask dug into the AU logo near midfield, and when he inhaled, he smelled the damp earth. But he couldn't lift his head. He couldn't feel anything. Except fear. They say your life flashes before your eyes in such moments. Zac flashed forward—to life in a wheelchair. "Jesus," he said quietly, "help me."

Aairon Savage remembers the silence. A stadium filled with eighty-seven thousand fans is not supposed to be so quiet. "You really could hear nature," Aairon says. "Everybody in the stadium was quiet, holding their breath. It felt like everything had paused except the wind."

Rodney Scott, lying underneath Zac, somehow had the presence of mind not to move. Doctors said later that Rodney's decision may have saved Zac's life. Dr. Goodlett and Coach Chizik knelt beside Zac. I followed them and stood a few steps behind the doctor as he asked Zac what he was feeling. Nothing.

In that moment a football game becomes insignificant. Only Zac is important. I'm thinking about his parents and other family up in the stands—how worried they must be wondering what's happening down here.

More minutes passed in silence. Zac and the Ole Miss player underneath him hadn't moved. The players on the field came together with heads bowed, and on the sidelines the rest of the team huddled in prayer. Finally, Dr. Goodlett motioned toward the sideline, and a stretcher was hurried onto the field. Zac said he was starting to get some feeling in his toes.

They stabilized Zac on a spine board, then Zac felt a finger and moved it. Maybe he would be okay. They rolled the stretcher toward the sideline, and the crowd began to stand and cheer.

"Let them see you move your hand," Dr. Goodlett said. Zac

lifted his right hand to give a thumbs-up, and the crowd cheered louder.

Jonna Chizik had come down from her seat in the stands and was waiting at the sideline with Cassandra and Donald. I knew she had been praying for Zac the whole time. She thought of every player on the team as her own son, and she was a prayer warrior. She prayed for each of them personally, especially when one was injured. "You're going to be fine," Jonna told Zac. "God has His hand on you."

She wasn't smiling as she spoke. These weren't her words of encouragement or a pep talk. Jonna was speaking what she knew to be the truth. Zac believed her, and I believed her, especially when she quoted Acts 11:21, and said, "Thousands will come to believe through this."

• • •

Jonna and I followed the ambulance and Zac's family to the hospital. When they brought Zac to a hospital room, his neck was braced, and feeling had returned to all his extremities. A nurse propped up his bed, and he asked her to turn on the television. We were leading 24–7 in the third quarter. A doctor stepped into the room, and Zac's first question was, "Will I be able to play football again?" Zac refused to be broken.

Cassandra felt tears in her eyes, but she knew what she had to say: "There's more to life than football."

Those are hard words for a determined person like Zac to accept. Harder words for a mother, who knows how much her son loves the game.

But the doctor did not say no. He explained that Zac's fifth cervical vertebra was fractured, and blood had collected behind the second vertebrae. He wanted him out of bed and moving around, but he would have to go to Birmingham for more tests and to be examined by another neurologist.

After the game, coaches and players and players' parents streamed in and out of the hospital, and Zac reflected on what had happened. "For me to go down like that in our home stadium and all those prayers going up right then," he said, "it showed me the power of prayer."

Zac also experienced love in a way he never imagined from people in the stands, his teammates, and his coaches. After he was transported to Birmingham, visitors continued to drop by. Coach Tommy Thigpen's wife, Jacinda, came up from Auburn. Lynn and Rick Trotter, Laurie McCain, and other parents came to support Zac and his family.

Lynn and Laurie told them about the prayers the mothers had lifted up early Saturday morning before the game—how they had all missed Tiger Walk because they so strongly felt the presence of the Holy Spirit. They were certain, now, they had been praying for Zac.

Then Cassandra told how God's grace had touched her. She almost never left her seat during games, but when we got the ball on offense, she thought she could get to the bathroom and back before Zac went back onto the field on defense. We lost the ball on downs while she was out of her seat, and Ole Miss took over. Two plays later Zac was injured. She missed the hit.

Zac left the hospital on Monday. His injury did not require surgery, but the road back to the football field would be long and difficult. He was wearing a huge two-piece neck brace on Tuesday when he told a crowd of media that he hoped to play again.

Cassandra prayed every day for God to heal Zac, and she cried for him every night. She walked the hallways of the hospital where she worked, wondering what she would do if God actually healed him. Would she let him play football again? Zac was a man, and he could make his own decisions, but Cassandra knew that if she told him not play football, Zac would walk away from it. Could she take that away from him? Take away the game that gave him so much joy? Take him away from something he had such passion for? The burden on her was so heavy, some days she could barely get out of bed.

Then one morning Cassandra was at work, and as she walked down the hall, she felt someone touch her shoulder. She turned but no one was there. Then she heard, just as clearly as if someone had been standing in front of her, "This is not about you." Cassandra had never heard voices before, but she knew instantly that this was the Holy Spirit. "This is about Me and Zac," she heard. "You told Zac when he got that diploma on his wall that he could make his own decisions. Remember? Well, this is between him and Me. It is not about you."

In that moment, Cassandra felt a weight lifted from her, a heavy load from her shoulders. She didn't have to make this decision. God was in control, and Cassandra would trust Him no matter what. No more fear. No more tears.

Thirteen days later the blood that had collected near Zac's spine was completely gone. "The doctor said he had never seen anything like that move on its own so fast," Zac said. "He didn't understand how it could have happened. I know that God gave me a second chance in life. Without completely putting me down, He gave me an eye-opener. He's telling me, 'I can heal you at any moment. I can be beside you at any moment.' And when I was lying on the ground paralyzed, He gave me the rest of my life, and I'm not taking that for granted."

Walking around campus with the brace, Zac stood out more than ever in his life. "God used me in different ways on campus," he says. "A lot of people asked me about my injury. Their questions helped me open up and not be afraid to speak my mind about what God was doing. That touched a lot of people in different ways. They tell me they're praying for me or send me Facebook messages. So since God gave me this opportunity, I try to use it to touch somebody's life every day—to encourage people to come closer to God."

Such a simple prayer: "Jesus, help me."

God says, "Okay, let Me find something you really love and put you out of it for a minute. Would you lose faith in Me?" I didn't lose faith in God. I let Him do His work.

ZAC ETHERIDGE

GOOD TO GREAT

JANUARY 2010

W E FINISHED THE 2009 season with an overtime win against Northwestern in the Outback Bowl, and on the way back to Auburn, Gene was already thinking about the next season and how to take the team to the next level. He met with his coaching staff and discussed what the players and they had done to become a good team with an 8–5 record. Then he said that in 2010 he wanted to lead us from being a good team to being a great team. He asked the coaches to read *Good to Great,* the best-selling business leadership book by Jim Collins.

The first line of *Good to Great* is, "Good is the enemy of great."

Too many companies, Collins wrote, settle for "good

enough," so they never achieve greatness.

If Collins had studied college football teams instead of companies, he might have written: "We don't have great football teams principally because we have good football teams." Many teams are satisfied with winning eight or nine games, which is good, so they don't do what is necessary to win twelve or thirteen or fourteen games, which is great.

"Greatness," Collins wrote, "is not a function of circumstance. Greatness is largely a matter of conscious choice, and discipline."

I began to think and pray about how the good-to-great theme could work in our spiritual life—how we could align our theme in Bible study and chapel time with Gene's theme for the team. Talking with a friend, I learned that Oswald Chambers, a Bible teacher and author of *My Utmost for His Highest,* had already made the connection, using almost the exact words nearly a century before Jim Collins wrote his book. "The greatest enemy of the life of faith in God is not sin," Chambers wrote, "but good choices which are not quite good enough. The good is always the enemy of the best."

Isn't that the truth?

Here's how I've witnessed *good* preventing *great.* One of our players sees me coming, and before I've even had a chance to speak, he says, "I'm good, Brother Chette. I'm good."

Or, more literally, he is saying, "I'm not a bad person. I'm a good guy. I'm not getting into real trouble. You don't need to be looking out for me."

But settling for "good enough" in our lives is the safest road to hell. We'll never be our best if we settle for good enough. Or worse, we will settle for the world's definition of good.

So how can we transform ourselves from good to great?

We cannot.

Only God can transform us. He changes us when we open our lives to Him. When we turn over everything to Him. When we stop worrying about what we do and focus instead on who we are.

I went to Coach Chizik's office one day, and they were in Bible study. He's right. This sport, this career, this focus is on football. But the coaches do a great job of balancing that, and it's refreshing to see. They do a great job as role models, teaching us the right thing, and what's important in life.

NEIL CAUDLE
QUARTERBACK AND HOLDER

SEND HELP!

MONAME BLANC MUST have been desperate. Maybe even dead.

Everything in the news on January 12, 2010, was about the earthquake in Port-au-Prince, where he lived—video images of collapsed and twisted buildings, bodies piled in the streets, parents desperately searching for lost children, and rescuers digging through the rubble for survivors. Dead or alive, Moname Blanc was somewhere among the ruins.

It was the second day of classes at Auburn, and his son Mike's cell phone had been vibrating since dawn with texts from teammates and friends who knew his father was in Haiti. Had Moname survived the earthquake? Had Mike heard from him?

Television news showed nothing but devastation. Thousands were dead. Maybe a million homes were destroyed. Building after building was flattened, even the presidential palace, crushing everyone inside.

Mike had tried to call his father again and again, but he couldn't get through to him or to any of his relatives in Haiti. There was no power in Port-au-Prince. No phone service. Mike watched and waited. Hoped and prayed.

In Miami, Mike's mother was filled with dread. She had left behind so many friends and family when she came to the United States. She could only wonder how many of them were trapped under rubble, waiting, hoping to be rescued.

Day after day Mike came to my office to pray. Every time, I asked him, "You okay?"

"Yeah," he said. "Good, man."

Sometimes I thought Mike was hiding his true feelings. His outlook after the initial shock was so positive, maybe too positive. But he was genuine, and his faith encouraged me. I began to believe that his dad was okay, and I told him so. "I'm praying for the blessing that he's all right," I said.

Mike's mother and siblings were more than six hundred miles away, so his teammates became his brothers. His coaches reached out to him every day. "I don't know where my head would have been," he says, "without their prayers and encouragement."

Finally, Mike's father called, and his description of the devastation confirmed everything we had seen in the news. The home his father had been living in was still standing, but a house down the street, where many of his cousins lived, had collapsed and killed them all. For the last few days Mike's father had slept outdoors, like so many thousands, afraid an aftershock might destroy the houses that were still standing. Bodies were being pushed to the sides of roads so vehicles could pass, and the smell of death hung over the city. There was nothing Mike could do.

A few days later Jonna Chizik stood at my office door and said she was about to book a flight to Haiti. The people down there needed help, and she was going. One thing I've learned about Jonna, when she says she's going to help somebody, she does it, especially if children are involved.

Jonna and Kristi Malzahn, wife of Coach Gus Malzahn, traveled to Haiti in February, and they saw everything: thousands of people roaming the streets with no place to live, contaminated water supplies, almost nothing to eat, orphanages overflowing, and so many homeless children looking for a shelter. Jonna and Kristi came back to Auburn believing that a group of our players could help rebuild an orphanage they had visited.

We had been talking since Jonna and Gene arrived in Auburn about the possibility of a mission trip for some of our players. My first idea had been to assist with tornado relief in north Alabama. But after returning from Haiti, Jonna thought an international trip might have a greater impact. I agreed. Ever since my first mission trip to Cuba many years ago, I have believed in the impact of going to places where we don't speak the language, where we can introduce the love of Christ by example to people who might not otherwise experience it.

I shared the idea with Jay Jacobs, and his initial concern was the players' safety. "But then, I have concerns when our tennis team goes to Oxford, Mississippi," Jay said. "That's my responsibility. At the same time, I often say that it's our responsibility to grow our student athletes physically, mentally, and spiritually—to broaden their vision beyond the classroom. They need to know what's going on in other parts of the world. To experience their pain and see that the life we have here isn't how life is everywhere."

So Jay was on board, and for several weeks we worked to organize a trip to Haiti for about a dozen players, coordinating with everybody from the athletic department to NCAA compliance officials. Three weeks before our departure time, just three months after the earthquake, we were not satisfied that the infrastructure in Haiti was safe enough to take our guys there. So we contacted Don Ankenbrandt at Alliance Ministries in Birmingham, who suggested that a trip to the Dominican Republic, which is east of Haiti on the same island of Hispaniola, could give us similar opportunities to serve and experience the needs of some of the poorest people in the Western Hemisphere.

Lakeba and I, along with several other chaperones, boarded a plane for the Dominican with Mike Blanc, Kodi Burns, Wes Byrum, Antoine Carter, Neil Caudle, Zac Etheridge, Nick Fairley, Mario Fannin, Lee Isom, Cam Newton, Ryan Pugh, Aairon Savage, Demond Washington, and Lee Ziemba.

COMPLETELY
BROKEN

MAY 2010

L EE ZIEMBA LOOKED around the Dominican village of
Aguas Negras and said, "The houses look like forts we
built when we were little kids."

He was right. Anybody could see that Aguas Negras was a
broken place. All along the dirt street, lumber scraps were nailed
to pieces of pressed cardboard, and tin sheets struggled to stand
up straight against a light breeze. These were people's homes.
Some residents had built walls by hammering old three-gallon
Crisco cans flat and then nailing them to boards they had pulled
from discarded shipping pallets.

We walked down the main street, and our guys didn't have
much to say at first. Several of our players had grown up in

poverty, and they had all seen homeless people on the streets back home. But nothing like this. Many of the women and children, however, smiled at us and nodded, welcoming us. We smiled back.

Lee, Neil, Ryan, and Wes broke away from our group to explore Aguas Negras on their own with a translator. None of them spoke Spanish or Creole, and despite their size, they soon began to feel vulnerable, uncomfortable, wondering if the people were watching them (they were). Walking up a side street they came upon a shack with a woman standing just inside the doorway. She smiled a sad smile behind lost eyes, and as they walked toward her, they realized she was standing in ankle-deep water—inside her home. Her name was Antonia, and her floor was several inches lower than the street grade. The whole thing was filled with stinking water. She had placed stones inside to step on when she moved about, but she had apparently given up on this. Her feet and ankles were as wrinkled as raisins, and she had sores up to her knees.

"She had this look," Neil told us later, "like she had nothing. Like we were looking into an empty person. She was so far gone. She was standing there, and she had lost all hope. I can't describe that look, but I can see it."

Antonia explained through the translator that her father was in the other room, in a corner, on a soaked and sagging mattress. A sheet hanging from the ceiling was the only wall. He was sick and slowly dying because he was always damp, and there was nothing anybody could do about it.

Whenever a storm brought rain or winds pushed water in from the sea, the water ran into her house. Ziemba asked if something could be done, and Brad, the missionary leading our group, explained, "When your thirty pesos for a day's work buys bread or milk or oatmeal, it seems less important to build your house up or do something else to keep the water out. Antonia is in that constant reality. This is actually a good time of year, but the rains will come again with the hurricane season."

"But her house is just broken," Ziemba said. "She's broken. The beams holding up the roof are just twigs, and when it rains the water all goes inside."

Aguas Negras means "black water," and in the Dominican Republic, "black water" is a polite term for sewage. At the edge of town, a few feet above sea level, was a sewage treatment facility that overflowed into the village when storms crossed the island. This little village of broken-down homes was at the mouth of a river that flowed down from the mountains and into what should have been a beautiful bay. But the river was filled with waste from neighbors upstream. At the water's edge, for as far as we could see in both directions, garbage was piled up two feet deep and fifty feet wide. Broken glass, cans, plastic bottles, rotten food—every kind of garbage was strewn around this landscape. Every wave that crashed against the trash washed a few pieces away and deposited more onto the beach.

For the first time in his life, Mike Blanc was standing on the island where his parents had been born, and he thought, *So this is what my family came from. This is why people die going from Haiti to Miami on little rafts.*

Muddy streams ran down every little street. The people rid their waste directly into creeks that ran through town to the ocean. The smell was awful. If the wind hit you in the face, the stench would burn your eyes.

The people of Aguas Negras are mostly Haitian refugees. If there are any untouchables in this world, these Haitians living in the Dominican Republic must be among their number. They escaped from Haiti to search for miserable jobs in the sugar cane fields. Then they were discarded, valued by their Dominican neighbors even less than the piles of garbage that surround them.

There weren't many men in the village. Many of the young women, Brad told us, were prostitutes. He said tourists from the United States and Europe made prostitution one of the most appealing professions in and around the nearby resort city of Puerto Plata. When children are born from those engagements, they are often abandoned to the street.

Yet these broken people in their broken village would show us glimpses of real hope and joy.

Going to the Dominican, I didn't even think about my injury anymore. Throughout that process I was just living life, enjoying every moment being able to walk again. To be able to go to the Dominican opened my eyes a whole lot. Opened my eyes to appreciate what we have here and love it. Seeing those kids. You just want to take everything you have and give it to them.

ZAC ETHERIDGE

SPIRIT ENABLED

SUDDENLY MIKE BLANC called out, "Bouyon!"

"Boo-what?" one of the guys responded.

"Bouyon," Mike said. "It smells like bouyon is being cooked. My mom makes that stuff." He waved at a woman on a small porch bending down over a steaming pot. "Are you making bouyon?" he asked her.

The woman smiled and waved Mike over, speaking what must have been Haitian Creole. Mike answered her, and suddenly the two of them were in a conversation that none of us understood. She shared a taste of her bouyon, the Haitian stew that Mike's mother had made almost every Saturday of his life. Other neighbors called out and walked over, and in a moment, Mike was no longer a stranger but a neighbor.

. . .

On that hot day in late spring, Pastor Jacob's little Haitian church was like a small oven with whitewashed walls and a corrugated tin roof held up by a frame of scavenged one-by-two-inch boards. The congregation sat on benches made with two-by-fours or in plastic chairs or on buckets. A fan in the corner stirred a little breeze. The pulpit was a beautiful mahogany podium with a clean white lace cloth draped over it.

There must have been about fifty people inside when Pastor Jacob introduced me to his congregation. I spoke for a few minutes, explaining a little about who we were and thanking them for their hospitality. Pastor Jacob translated my words into Creole. The adults listened politely, and the children squirmed. I knew I didn't have their attention. It's hard to concentrate when it's so hot and the speaker isn't even speaking your language. Then I mentioned that the parents of one of our players were Haitian and that Mike Blanc spoke Creole. Pastor Jacob insisted that I invite Mike to the pulpit.

Mike stepped up and placed his big hands on the pulpit and began to speak. Instantly, every child settled down. Every eye in the room turned toward Mike. I did not understand his words, but they did. I could see in his expression the love he shared with these people, and I could see that he was sharing with them what Christ meant to him.

More people squeezed into the little room, standing all the way around the walls, and at the door I could see Ziemba and some of our guys looking in, watching their brother with a new admiration.

The Bible says that at Pentecost the disciples "began to speak with other tongues as the Spirit enabled them" and "each one of them was hearing them speak in his own language."

For a few minutes a village of Haitian immigrants, the poorest of the poor in this world, listened as an American football player spoke the gospel in their own language. He thanked them for their hospitality and for the food they had shared. When Mike finished, the room was filled with laughter, tears, joy, and understanding.

Mike insisted later, when he told us what he had said, "That wasn't my mom's Creole. She would have hit me across the head real quick."

No, that was the Holy Spirit's Creole.

We went over there thinking we were going to impact the people there. At the end of the day, they really impacted us. They helped us realize how much we have and how thankful we should be. They don't have anything, but they're the happiest people in the world. They have all they need to be happy. They really opened our eyes.

ANTOINE CARTER
DEFENSIVE LINEMAN

DANGEROUS
UNSELFISHNESS

W E HAVE TO do something," Lee Ziemba said when we
gathered outside the little church. "We have to help
these people."

Brad said we needed to see more before we talked about
how we could help, and he had a construction day planned for
later in the week. This day we would go out to the edge of the
village to play ball. We had brought a few things with us, so we
walked down the street with Antoine bouncing a basketball,
Wes carrying a soccer ball and a baseball, Kodi with another
baseball and glove, Lee Isom with another soccer ball, and all of
us carrying backpacks filled with candy. One by one, children
fell in behind us like we were pied pipers, begging for a ball to

bounce or pitch or kick. There was such a variety, and all of them beautiful. Some had skin as black as Bibles; others were much lighter and European looking.

By the time we reached the trash dump, which was the children's playground (and for some a source of food and shelter), dozens of kids were running all around us, laughing and throwing balls. Then one of our guys broke out the candy, and even more children came running our way. Some of the smaller ones clung tightly to us, and when the candy ran out, Ryan put one of the children onto his back. Within seconds every player had two or three kids begging for rides, and their laughter echoed across the dump.

Brad explained some of the consequences of what we were seeing: "Where we see a high concentration of kids, good and bad people find out about that, and both try to create opportunity—some for children, and some for themselves. That's reality here. It's tough for us to see it on regular basis. But many of these parents are desperate. They may engage their children in a working arrangement or send them to work camps in other countries. Many of the girls and boys end up in prostitution, and there isn't much we can do to help them."

I looked at these children and I couldn't help thinking somewhat angrily of men somewhere across the waters who had come to this place seeking their own pleasure and had left behind so much misery.

• • •

I was eight years old the first time God answered my prayer. We lived in a little house at the end of the road, off in the woods, and one night my parents went out for the evening. They told my other older brothers to look after me and my brother Percy, who was six, while they were out. Mom and Dad hadn't been gone ten minutes when Calvin Jr., the oldest, looked at me and said, "You and Percy don't get into any trouble. We're going out."

I panicked. They couldn't leave us all alone!

"But Mama said for you to look after us!" I cried.

"You'll be okay," Calvin Jr. said, and just like that, my brothers were out the door. Gone.

I locked the door and didn't look out the window. It was so dark outside, and I was so alone and Percy was so little. I fell onto the sofa and started crying and praying. "Please, God, please, please send them back," I cried. "Oh, please don't leave us here all alone." Then Percy started crying too.

I don't know how long I prayed, whether it was five minutes or thirty minutes. All I know is that, while I was praying, I heard a knock at the door. I stopped crying and didn't move. I didn't know who was there, and I couldn't let them hear me. Finally Calvin Jr. shouted, "Unlock the door!" Relief flooded over me, and I ran to the door and unlocked it.

"We changed our mind," Calvin Jr. said as soon as the door opened. "We decided to come back." And that's what he believed. They just decided to come back. But I knew different. God had answered my prayer, and it changed me. He had brought them back. When you're eight years old and you experience something like that, the memory becomes part of your foundation—something you go back to and build on for the rest of your life.

I had cried out to God for my brothers to come home, and He gave me something even more precious: the knowledge that He heard my prayers and had been with me all along.

In Aguas Negras, parents don't come back. In the muddy streets, orphans roam barefoot. In the early morning, children scavenge the dump for anything to eat. In the evening they prostitute themselves for a few pesos. All day long they wipe their runny noses, a symptom of intestinal parasites. Everyone in the community has worms. There is no indoor plumbing, so they drink from the creek that carries away their waste.

I wonder what the children of Aguas Negras pray for. For their parents to come back? For their older siblings to protect them? For food to eat or a dry place to sleep? How long before they are as empty as Antonia, the woman in the doorway of her flooded house? What do they believe about God? Why would they believe anything good?

. . .

In his final sermon, on the night before he was killed, Dr. Martin Luther King Jr. spoke about the Jericho Road and the good Samaritan. When faced with an injured man on the side of the road, Dr. King said, "The first question that the Levite [a religious leader] asked was, 'If I stop to help this man, what will happen to me?' But then the good Samaritan came by. And he reversed the question: 'If I do not stop to help this man, what will happen to him?'" Dr. King challenged his hearers to "develop a kind of dangerous unselfishness" like the good Samaritan.

I saw that spirit in our football players, running around a

Dominican trash dump and playing with a bunch of children, never stopping to consider what might happen to the children or themselves. They just played. At that moment every child was smiling, and their joy was overflowing onto us. Nobody wanted to leave that trash dump. We thought we had come to bring a moment of happiness into the lives of downcast people. Instead, the children were sharing an inexpressible joy that we would talk about deep into the night.

Back at our hotel, we wondered what we could do for the people of Aguas Negras to relieve even a bit of their misery. We couldn't build an orphanage for all the children, and we couldn't create a system for the people of Aguas Negras to have jobs. But in a day and a half our group could rebuild Antonia's house to make it dry, and we were ready to go to work.

Brad, however, advised against our swooping in like a North American Santa Claus and solving problems. He and his wife, Brooke, had been living among the people, and he told us, "These people are so without hope. They're living in an unending spiral downward from generation to generation. Many of the adults grew up on the streets themselves, resorting to prostitution in exchange for shelter. Our task is to help them break that cycle and become self-sufficient. You can rebuild one home for one family, but when you come back in a year, it will look just like it does today unless you help people see themselves in God's image. That is a deep, deep crevice in life and in culture. That's why we require that they participate and take some responsibility, but they are so oppressed and so hopeless in their spirits, it is hard for them to follow through on things like that."

So we couldn't even build a little house for a desperate family. But like Ziemba said, we had to do *something*. We couldn't just pray for them and then go home. Brad reminded us that we would be working with the people the next day to help them build a church that would serve many needs in the community. He also told us about a Georgia Tech graduate who had recently discovered terracotta water filters used by people in Tanzania to transform the dirtiest water into safe, drinkable water. One filter cleans five gallons a day—enough for a family—and a filter lasts five years or longer. A nonprofit organization in the Dominican Republic was making the filters available for thirty dollars each. Brad said we could buy filters for some of the people of Aguas Negras.

We wanted to do something big, maybe something grand to change the lives of the people we had met. Brad was suggesting something that appeared small. We wouldn't even be around when the filters were delivered. But our gift could change lives. A few gallons of clean water every day would save the lives of many babies and children and allow many more to live without intestinal parasites.

That trip was my changing point. More than
that. There's a point in somebody's life when
you have to hit the reset button and gather
everything again. That trip was a lot of people's
reset buttons.

CAM NEWTON

QUARTERBACK

I had a tough time when I came back. You go there and see kids with no clothes eating garbage, then you come here and watch people waste so much. Down there twelve- and fourteen-year-old girls have babies and no help from anybody. I had a tough time dealing with that. I take so much for granted when they have so little.

WES BYRUM
KICKER

EVERYBODY IS SHOT

SUMMER 2010

I THOUGHT I was too young for hip replacement surgery, but a few weeks after we returned from the Dominican Republic, I knew it was time. I had actually started down this road more than thirty years earlier, and finally the pain was more than I could bear.

You've seen a playground carousel, the big, round platform with bars to hold onto. Kids push it around and then jump on while it spins. Now imagine that carousel under the control of a bunch of twelve-year-old boys and their older brothers, with no adults in sight. Ever wonder how fast a carousel will turn? We did.

When I was a kid, there was a park in Douglasville where we played football and baseball, and there were swings and a carousel that we had long outgrown. One afternoon we decided to test the speed limit of that little merry-go-round. I sat down in the middle while my cousin Cleve and my brothers held onto the bars and started running. The faster they ran, the dizzier we all got. Finally they gave it one last push, and I looked up at the clouds spinning in a tight circle above me. I slid down a little, with my feet hanging off the edge as I whirled, but somebody didn't move out of the way when they gave that final push, and my leg slammed into him while the platform kept spinning beneath me. A metal bar crashed against my thigh and swung me hard toward the edge until I rolled off and fell onto the ground. Something moved deep in my right hip. I knew it wasn't natural, but it wasn't all that painful. Not yet.

I stood up and staggered a little, dizzy. We were all dizzy. Then somebody suggested we ride to Cleve's house, and I didn't have any trouble on my bike until I turned into Cleve's yard. The back wheel slid out from under me and I laid it down, but when I put my right foot down to keep from falling, my hip gave way, and I collapsed on the ground. I was a little confused, because my leg still didn't hurt that much. I just couldn't stand up. So I sat in Cleve's driveway and watched the other guys play football until dark, when Cleve's dad came home and put me in the back of his pickup truck and took me home.

My dad didn't mean to hurt me. But when you have seven boys, somebody's always coming home with bumps and bruises, and you can't haul them off to the emergency room unless it's something really serious. When he got home, he walked back to the bedroom, where my mom had put me in the bed, and he started his diagnosis.

"What happened?" he asked.

I explained the playground and the bike and said I couldn't put any weight on my leg.

"How bad does it hurt?"

"Not that bad," I said. "I just can't stand on it."

"You think it's out of the socket?"

"I don't know."

"Let me see," he said, and he put his big hands around my ankle and lifted my leg straight up. Something like a hand grenade exploded in my hip, and fire raced all the way into my chest and down my arms. I thought I was going to throw up. Instead, I screamed. I grabbed the sheets and squeezed hard, with tears on my face. Then Pop pushed my knee toward my chest. I may have passed out. I don't remember much after that.

I'm not sure whether the bone broke on the merry-go-round, falling off my bike, or when Pop started pushing it around, but the surgeon put three metal pins near the top of my femur. He said that the bone would grow over the pins in time, and I would be 100 percent again. He was right. After two years, in my junior year at Douglas County High School, I was finally playing football again.

But deep inside, where nobody could see and I could not feel, the bone was slowly dying. Those pins in the top of my thighbone were blocking some of the blood flow to the bone and cartilage cells around them, starving the cells at the top of my femur. After twenty-five years the ball flattened out. They call it avascular necrosis, and the hip is especially susceptible.

· · ·

The lawn chairs looked so inviting. All I wanted was to sit down for a few minutes. My right hip was tired and hurting, and the chairs were right there. In the days when Coach Tuberville allowed the public to attend practice, a group of local retirees brought lawn chairs almost every day and set them up along the sidelines. If I could just take the weight off for a little bit . . .

But coaches don't sit down during practice, and neither do players. They may take a knee, but they don't sit. I'm neither a coach nor a player, but if I'm going to relate to them, I have to stand with them. No sitting.

I remembered a scene from the movie *Black Hawk Down*, where a convoy of Army Rangers in Humvees is under attack and taking heavy casualties. The soldier driving one of the Humvees is killed, so the colonel leading the Rangers turns to a soldier and says, "Get in that truck and drive."

"But I'm shot, Colonel," the soldier says.

"Everybody's shot," the colonel barks back. "Get in and drive!"

Everybody is shot. Every player and coach. My father and mother, my six brothers, my wife, even my three children. You've been shot. We're all bleeding in places no one else sees. We're all in pain. We all need help.

Despite the pain, sometimes we have to get in the truck and drive.

I stood on the sidelines for a few more years, and the discomfort grew to the point that I had to keep pacing to hold back the pain. I couldn't play racquetball anymore. Then I couldn't run. I couldn't go outside with my children and play basketball and volleyball. I had to tell them no. Finally, I couldn't even go for walks with Lakeba.

So in the summer of 2010, I was rolled out of surgery with a new artificial hip. A nurse came to my room to show me a button I could push whenever I felt pain, and she said it would deliver anesthesia quickly. She left the room, and I immediately pushed the button. Then I waited, but the pain didn't go away. I pushed the button again. Still nothing.

"Lakeba," I said, "I don't think this thing is working." Lakeba said she'd call the nurse, but I said no, and I pushed the button again. Late in the evening the pain was so bad I could barely stand it. I told Lakeba to go home and take care of the kids, but what I really wanted was to curl up and be alone. She left, and I tried to roll onto my side. That's when I realized my left leg was numb. The pain block was on the wrong side.

The God of all comfort felt like He was a million miles away, but I prayed anyway. Somewhere in the night I fell asleep and experienced peace.

Practice started a few weeks after my surgery, and I was limping around with a cane. Gene told me to go home. In a nice way, of course. He wanted me to take care of myself. I sat in a chair on the sidelines, and players asked me what I was doing at practice. Maybe it was pride, especially around these young guys. I wanted to show them how tough I was, and it hurt. I held in my frustration until I got home. Then I went to bed and lay there, weak and irritable. Lakeba and our children were so much more patient with me than I was with them.

I had forgotten the story in the Bible about the lame man whose four friends carried him down the road to be healed by Jesus. When they arrived at the crowded house and couldn't get inside, they carried their friend to the roof, cut a hole in it, and lowered him to Jesus' feet.

These players and coaches had carried their friends literally and figuratively down their broken roads, and I knew they would do anything for me. I threw away the cane before I should have—I couldn't look at it anymore—then limped around the Athletic Complex and down to the practice field. My hidden pain was finally in the open, and my friends and family helped bear my burden.

We have so many valley experiences, and we're in the valley for so long. Then all of a sudden He'll bring us to the mountaintop. We know, of course, there will be another valley. We also know that Jesus has come down from the mountaintop. He's standing beside us in the valley. He's in our rocking boat. He's always there. We don't have to go to the mountaintop to find Him.

JAY JACOBS
DIRECTOR OF ATHLETICS

CONFIDENCE,
NOT
OVERCONFIDENCE

SEPTEMBER 3, 2010

C URTIS LUPER THOUGHT we should sing. Our running
backs coach had a beautiful deep voice, and his father
was a pastor, so he felt comfortable leading our players and
coaches (who don't have such beautiful voices). "But the church
is forgiving," Luper said.

The entire team and staff were eating dinner together on Friday
night before the first game of the 2010 season in a banquet room
at the Renaissance Hotel in Montgomery. It's a pregame tradition
that began many years ago, and after dinner I deliver a message.

Luper thought if we could get the guys to sing a couple of
songs before I spoke, it might help them focus. After dinner he
walked up to the front of the room and sang a chorus of "One

More Time," then we joined in: "One more time. One more time. He allowed us to come together one more time."

We were a pretty rough bunch singing. A lot of the guys were self-conscious about singing in front of their teammates and coaches, so they didn't put much behind it, and in that big room our voices kind of drifted out into space. Then Luper picked up the pace with "Oh Happy Day," which they sang slightly more enthusiastically after the big meal.

Next, Lee Ziemba, our senior left tackle, prayed for us, as he would at every chapel service throughout the season, before turning it over to me for the message.

As much as possible, I wanted to build my chapel messages around Gene's theme of Good to Great. From the first day of practice in August, Gene had been stressing Good to Great. He reminded the players that they had improved from five wins in 2008 to eight wins in 2009, and that was good, but not great. "We changed the way we thought just enough to win three more games," he said.

We had lost three games by a touchdown or less—three games that would have transformed our 2009 season from good to great. "We didn't win eleven," he said, "because we didn't entirely change the way we think. We were good enough to win eight games. We didn't change enough to win eleven. More change has got to happen."

I looked down at my G2G bracelet, just like the ones players and coaches had been wearing since early August, and I said the first step on the road to greatness is to have confidence without becoming overconfident. Confidence.

I told of the story of Jericho, where God instructed Joshua and the Israelites to march around the city seven times, and then blow their horns, and the city walls would fall down. Joshua followed the plan, despite its lack of common sense, because he had confidence that God would, indeed, knock down the walls. The people saw Joshua's confidence, and they followed him as he led them around the city again and again. And when they blew their horns, the Lord, indeed, knocked down the walls.

Gene Chizik's quiet confidence in the Lord reminded me of Joshua. The players and coaches must have known about his record as a head coach at Iowa State, and maybe that concerned some of them. Then they saw his confidence, his strength, and his integrity, and they believed he would lead them to victory.

Ask any player, "What did you come to Auburn to do?" and he'll answer, "Win." "Win what?" "Win championships."

But there is a line between confidence and overconfidence that you cannot afford to cross. Soon after the great victory over Jericho, Joshua sent spies to check out a little town up the road called Ai. The spies came back and told Joshua, "You don't need to worry about that little place. Don't even bother sending the whole army. Just send a couple thousand men up there, and they'll take that town easy." In fact, the English translation of Ai is "ruin."

So Joshua did as they recommended and sent just three thousand men up to Ai, and the next thing he knew that little town was routing his men, chasing them out, shooting them in the back, embarrassing them and the nation before the world.

Every year one good football team or another encounters its

Ai, whether it's Michigan against Appalachian State, Oklahoma against Kansas State, or Florida against Ole Miss.

We did not want to start the season against Arkansas State overconfident.

More important, we don't want to become spiritually overconfident. Too often college students think they can go out with friends on Saturday and not have much to drink, and then they end up drunk. Or maybe they can watch a movie they've heard about, the one they know they shouldn't be watching, but they're confident that it's just a peek. And before they know it, they're sitting in front of a computer and watching porn.

Spiritual overconfidence. We think we can handle anything we meet along the way.

We gain confidence and avoid overconfidence through prayer—confidence to do little things like sing in front of your teammates, and confidence to reveal your pain, knowing your brothers will share your load.

The last thing we do on Friday night, after team dinner, chapel, and team meetings is come together for a time of prayer. By that time the night has grown long, and players are tempted to go to their rooms to relax. Instead, they come together for an hour.

On the first Friday night of the 2010 season, however, the seniors called a players-only meeting, something they would do the night before every game in 2010. By then I knew we would lose even more of our crowd, so I prayed as they filed into the hallway for a large group of them to come together in prayer at the end of the night.

On Friday night you experience that intimate moment where you see the Spirit in the circle. We have busy, hectic lives. But on Friday we can go to a special place where God knows your heart and touches your spirit. College men linking up and singing where the whole purpose is glorifying God.

AAIRON SAVAGE
DEFENSIVE BACK

NOBODY WAS
LUKEWARM

SEPTEMBER 3, 2010

O VER THE COURSE of the season, the public and the media would attach negative labels ("dirty" was their favorite) to some of the players who were strong leaders on Friday night.

God loves those guys. I mean, He *really* loves them.

They were often the first to find me after practice and say, "Hey, Brother Chette, I need to come see you." And on Friday night, as soon as the players-only meeting ended, they were the guys who stood in the hallway and told their teammates, "Let's go. Get on in here for prayer."

Those guys knew their need for that prayer time, and they coveted their teammates' prayers for themselves.

Jesus told a parable about a Pharisee who went up to the temple and prayed, thanking God for making him a righteous man who tithed and fasted and avoided unclean people. Beside the Pharisee stood a tax collector who beat on his chest and cried out, "God, be merciful to me, the sinner!" The second man, Jesus said, walked home justified rather than the "righteous" Pharisee.

I think the guys on our team with reputations are attracted to me because they know I walked a troubled road when I was their age. They know about my negative reputation when I came to Auburn as a young man and that my coaches gave up all hope for me. And they know Christ changed my life.

These guys are anything but lukewarm. Misunderstood, but not lukewarm. Christ looks for people like them—people with a history and a reputation.

During the off-season I often meet with players on Sunday afternoons for a worship service. One Sunday in the spring I was preaching, and I saw a player who I knew the coaches were struggling with. I was talking about how Christ reached out to the misunderstood, and I looked at this player and said, "People just like you," and I used his name.

"What?" he asked. He was clearly confused and wondered why I would point him out.

"Christ reached out to people just like you," I repeated, again using his name. "You are the most misunderstood player on this team. Other people look at you and see a young man who doesn't have it all together personally, and they wonder if you'll make it. I don't see that. I see a tremendous athlete who is misunderstood—the same kind of man Christ surrounded Himself with."

The following Sunday afternoon that player was the first to arrive and help me set up for Bible study. He hadn't made a miraculous change in his lifestyle from Sunday to Sunday, but he came by my office twice that week to talk. He knew, just like they all know, that when he came to my office, I was going to open the Bible. I always open the Word with them. It draws some in and it drives some away. The Bible says God will "spit out" the luke-warm from His mouth. The Latin word that we translate "spit" is actually *vomere,* or "vomit"—a disgusting rejection.

I didn't see any lukewarm guys coming out of the players meeting that night. They were pumped up and ready to pray, and on the first Friday night of the 2010 season, we had to find more chairs for the prayer room. Nearly every player came in.

Church should be about fellowship—a place to rest in the Lord with other believers. But on Sunday mornings after games, I could hardly get myself out of bed. So Friday night chapel and prayer meeting was my church.

The night before a game can be such a stressful time, Brother Chette's message helped me put all those things away and reflect on the Lord. I put away thoughts and concerns about tomorrow.

Sometimes he tied his message to football, but I liked it better when he didn't. Everything we did all week long—all our activities revolved around football. Football was the structure of our lives.

I wanted Friday night to be God's times.

LEE ZIEMBA

SERVANT LEADERS

BACK IN MAY, on the third night of our trip to the Dominican Republic, Lakeba and I had made plans for a time of prayer and communion with the players on a nearby mountain. But it rained all day, canceling our construction and forcing us to move communion inside. We thought we would be in the hotel, but our host, Brad, told us he knew a man who owned a restaurant with a large room on the second floor.

After dinner we went to the room above the restaurant, and the open windows caught a breeze and the sounds of the street below. The room was just big enough for all of us to set up chairs in a circle. We talked about the things we had seen in our three days, and then we prayed one by one around the circle for

Antonia in her wet house, the children at the dump, for Mike Blanc's father and all the people of Haiti, and for teammates and family back home. We thanked God for the opportunity to see the most vulnerable of God's children with fresh eyes.

After more than two hours of prayer, Lakeba and I served the Lord's Supper. We had planned this ahead of time without telling anyone, but we had not anticipated being in a borrowed "upper room." The setting felt almost biblical as we broke bread and shared juice—the body and blood of our Lord. Finally, we took a pan of water and prepared to wash the feet of our friends. Again, Lakeba and I had planned this in advance, but we never know how God is going to work.

Of the four gospel writers, John is the only who tells of Jesus washing His disciples' feet, which must have been sweaty and dirty after walking the streets of Jerusalem in their sandals. By His act, Jesus was serving the disciples and showing them how He wanted them to serve. "Now that I, your Lord and Teacher, have washed your feet, you also should wash one another's feet. I have set you an example that you should do as I have done for you."

Each year we select one or two guys, usually seniors but not always our on-field leaders, to lead our Friday night prayer meetings. Technically it's my choice, but I respond to leadership in the prayer room from year to year. The players' choices can almost always be described as servant leaders. Aairon Savage and Neil Caudle were chosen in 2010.

Aairon was like a son to me, and I don't say that lightly. He had been recruited as a high school senior back in 2004 by Gene Chizik, who was our defensive coordinator then, and he came looking for me as soon as he arrived on campus. Aairon had grown up in church, and he was seeking a mature relationship with Christ.

When Aairon tore his ACL just before his junior year, he thought he would never play again. His complete recovery from that injury, he said, "couldn't have been anything but Christ." Then he injured his Achilles tendon and lost another season. By that time he and I had spent many hours together in the hospital, and because of his injuries he had not traveled with the team for two years. Yet he never lost his connection to his teammates and coaches. He was in my office several times every week. He came to Bible study and FCA meetings, and he never missed a scheduled workout with Coach Yox. Ryan Pugh said Aairon is "the epitome of what a college athlete should be," and Aairon's teammates agreed. He was a natural leader for our prayer meeting.

When Cam Newton arrived, and won the starting quarterback position, Neil had a final chance to transfer to another school, where he likely would have started. "It was tough to stick around sometimes," he says. "When I got here I thought I'd be winning championships and MVPs. Instead, my role was reduced to holding for kicks. But every time I prayed about, it felt like God wanted me to stay here." Ask any player from 2010, and he will tell you that Neil's leadership off the field and in the prayer room was a key to the cohesion of the team all season.

The most important characteristic of our team leaders is

trust. Players trusted Neil and Aairon. In the prayer room, guys were sharing their deepest hurts and concerns, sometimes tearfully. In those extremely vulnerable moments, they lifted their hurting brothers up and bonded so tightly that nothing happening on a football field could divide them.

What establishes Aairon as a leader? He's a guy who not only comes to prayer meeting and participates, but who lives the lifestyle. Aairon is who he is. He hasn't changed, and he is not going to change. He's a good person. Everybody sees that. He has persevered through all kinds of injuries. Guys respect that from a player's standpoint. That's why guys like Aairon step into a leadership role and others look up to them.

NEIL CAUDLE

LEAN ON ME

SEPTEMBER 8, 2010

O N WEDNESDAY AFTERNOON, just four days after we opened the season with a 52–26 win over Arkansas State, we loaded onto buses and headed up the road to Starkville, Mississippi, for a Thursday night game against Mississippi State. The hotel where we stayed in Starkville, and the banquet room where we ate supper Wednesday night, were smaller than the Renaissance. But there was one important advantage: acoustics.

After supper, Coach Luper got up to lead the singing, and with backup quarterback Barrett Trotter on the guitar, they led us in "One More Time." We sounded better than we had that first Friday, but still not good. Barrett suggested to Luper that we try some songs other than gospel standards, and they decided to sing "Lean on Me," the Bill Withers classic that was a hit when my older brothers were in high school.

Many times since our undefeated 2004 season, people have told me we need to try to capture the spirit of that team. They tell me, "Y'all need to sing 'Hard Fighting Soldier' again." But that was another journey. Another road. We can't go back to the past. If you're focused on Jesus, you're not looking at the past. You're not looking at anything but Him. Just trusting Him. Every team has its own spirit, and we pray every year that Christ will reveal Himself in and through that team spirit.

Something special happened when we sang "Lean on Me." The players and coaches were singing to each other with passion. We had 140 people squeezed into a room big enough for 90, and we were rocking the walls. "Just call on me, brother, when you need a friend!" We had no idea how often we would be calling out that line over the next four months.

Lee Ziemba led us in prayer, and then I offered a message on faith, another necessary characteristic in the transformation from good to great. Faith allows you to put yourself under the direction of a leader, to lean on someone else who will show you the way to greatness. Noah's faith led to his obedience in the building of the ark, following God's specific instructions. To go from good to great, you have to keep your assignment. Just like coaches give assignments that, when followed, lead to success, God gives us assignments that we have to complete. Sometimes those assignments seem to make about as much sense as building an ocean liner in the desert. And then the rain begins to fall.

On Thursday night the offense got off to another good start, scoring seventeen points in the first half. Then punt, punt, punt. Nothing like the week before, when they had poured it on for fifty-two points. "We didn't score another point," Cam said after the game. "We started off on fire, but we put our defense in some binds."

The defense, which had given up twenty-six points to Arkansas State, tightened and held Mississippi State to fourteen, so we came away with a 17–14 win. In the locker room after the game, Coach Chizik talked about how everyone in the room would rely on each other from week to week, offense one week, defense the next. Then he called Curtis Luper over to lead the team in singing "Lean on Me," which we sang even louder than the night before.

We had found our song and our theme: "We all need somebody to lean on."

On Friday night during prayer time, players see God working in each other's lives, no matter where they're from, no matter what position they play, how much they play. It's even ground. You can feel the spirit of the Lord in there because it's genuine. It isn't something they're forced to do. Not something mandatory. The guys are speaking from the heart, and it really moved me as a coach.

Very seldom as a coach have I had the chance to see that side of a football player, where he's opening his heart—to see players' tears shared in the emotion of understanding what another teammate is going through. It's beautiful, then, to see these players praying individually for each other—the starting quarterback praying for a walk-on defensive back and his family, guys from such different backgrounds coming together in prayer. It was the glue to our football team.

TROOPER TAYLOR

ASSISTANT COACH, 2009-12

NO CONDEMNATION

SEPTEMBER 17, 2010

RICK BURGESS KNEW we didn't do pep talks at Friday night chapel. His son Blake was a redshirt freshman center in 2010. When I asked Rick to speak to us the night before the Clemson game, he said he knew not to talk about football. (We usually invite a guest or two to speak at chapel during the season. Players say they like hearing other speakers.)

Rick earns a living by being funny on the radio. But our guys weren't looking for funny. They'd come to expect our chapel speaker to deliver the Word, and Rick didn't let them down.

Rick had been at a conference in Nashville two years earlier when he received word that his two-year-old son, Bronner, had fallen into the swimming pool at their home and drowned.

144

"Nothing is more humbling," he said, "than when you walk into a children's hospital and your wife is holding the lifeless body of one of your children. That's when you go to God and say, 'I can't do this!' And God says, 'I know you can't. I will.'"

At that point it would have been easy for the Burgess family to start asking questions, placing blame, and making condemnations. Other families have been broken by similar tragedies. Not the Burgesses. Rick says his greatest comfort in the death of his child was knowing that Bronner was in the care "of the only Father who loves him more than I do." With that knowledge, the Burgesses made a commitment to follow a path that would make a positive impact in God's kingdom.

When Friday night came, Rick stood in front of the team and opened his Bible to Romans 8, which he called, "the greatest pep talk of all time, because it starts out by telling us, 'There is now no condemnation for those who are in Christ.'"

No condemnation. Imagine that. Only life and peace.

We criticize so quickly. I've heard people fuss at Rick on the air because they thought he wasn't funny enough, and some of the radio sports talk shows offer almost nothing but condemnation because they take the games so seriously.

"For a lot of people in our state," Rick says, "Auburn football is an idol. Alabama football is an idol. Well, let me tell you something. Football is a great game, but it's a lousy god."

Idols lead to failure, and failure leads to condemnation. Encouragement, on the other hand, and forgiveness lead to strength. And it was only God's strength that allowed Rick and his family to survive a broken road that none of us should have to walk. That's the story he wanted to share with our players.

"You may know how to win," he told us, "but do you have victory? You know, our biggest problem is not with Clemson tomorrow. It's our eternity. It's our sin. Until you get this resolved in your life, you'll never be the player you could be. Never be the man you could be. If you go out onto the football field tomorrow and have the adulation of eighty-seven thousand people but don't have the approval of an audience of One, it's meaningless.

"My son Blake wants to play center, but if he doesn't have an impact for the kingdom, what does it matter? Who remembers who the Auburn center was ten years ago?"

Every man in the room was focused on Rick, who doesn't speak without a time of decision, a challenge to his audience to commit or recommit their lives to Christ.

Then he reminded us again that our God is a God of forgiveness, and there is no condemnation to those who are in Christ. He prayed for us all, and as we dismissed from dinner, a big group of guys crowded around Rick with questions. He stayed for our prayer meeting, and afterward more players spent time with him until about eleven o'clock. This man who had been broken was showing the scars of his brokenness, sharing the source of his strength, and guiding young men toward a new direction for their lives.

• • •

On Saturday night when the Clemson game ended, our fans danced in the aisles. On the field, Josh Harris hurt for

Matt Skinner. "You want to win every game," Josh says, "but you never wish bad on anybody."

Josh was our long snapper. Skinner was Clemson's long snapper.

The game had gone into overtime, tied 24–24, and on our first possession we had kicked a thirty-nine-yard field goal to take a three-point lead. Josh, Neil Caudle, and Wes Byrum had made a perfect snap, hold, and kick.

Then Clemson got the ball and pushed down to our eight-yard line, in front of the student section, where they stalled. Their kicker, Chandler Cantazaro, came on and made the easy field goal to tie the game again and keep the overtime going. But there was a penalty on the field. Matt Skinner had flinched a little just before he snapped the ball, and the referee had dropped a flag. Clemson was hit with a five-yard penalty. Pushed back to the thirteen-yard line, the kick was still a chip shot, but this time Cantazaro hooked it to the left, and in an instant the game was over.

The band played and fans waved and screamed. Our guys rushed onto the field, jumping and laughing and hugging. But Josh was looking for number 71 in white and orange. He wanted to offer consolation—to share Matt Skinner's pain. He never found him. Skinner had gone straight to the locker room.

The margin of error for a long snapper is incredibly small. Josh and Neil knew, for example, that Neil would always set up exactly seven yards and one foot behind the line of scrimmage. That allowed Josh to spiral the ball to Neil so that the laces were already facing the goalpost when they hit Neil's hands. Neil could place the ball without having to turn it again, just in time for Wes to make the kick. They worked on the snap and placement thousands of times in practice.

"I've had guys snap rockets that were too tough to handle," Neil says. "But you don't want soft either. As soon as I call for the ball, I know exactly when it will hit my hands. I can do it with my eyes closed—hold out my hands and Josh will hit them just right. Sometimes in practice I did it with one hand."

Matt Skinner and his holder, Michael Wade, surely had the same trusting relationship. But in one instant, one flinch, the game was lost.

A huge group of players and coaches gathered in a circle at midfield for a prayer before we ran to the locker room, where Coach Chizik always calls on me to pray before he speaks to the players. Except this time he was so excited, he forgot and just started talking. I didn't want to embarrass him by interrupting.

A couple of assistants were bolder. "Hey, Coach, Coach," they said, and Gene stopped and turned. "Coach, Brother Chette's gotta pray."

"Oh, man, I forgot," Gene said, laughing, and he looked at me. "Brother Chette . . ." Then he paused and said, "No, I tell you what. Let me do it."

I love it! I thought. These guys all are so into the Spirit, they even turn our missteps into opportunities to lift up each other. And through his prayer Gene invited the Holy Spirit to minister to me.

Listening to Gene pray instead of speaking the prayer

myself, my thoughts went to the long snapper in the next locker room—the relationships he had with the other players and coaches—and I hoped there would be no condemnation, that his teammates would lift him up and pour out their forgiveness so he could walk out to the bus for the trip home feeling more love than he could imagine.

"There is now no condemnation for those who are in Christ."

HIS STRENGTH

OCTOBER 8, 2010

O N THE FRIDAY night before the Kentucky game, I preached on Ephesians 6:10–17 for the first time since 2004. "Put on the full armor of God, so that you will be able to stand firm against the schemes of the devil." It's a passage many pastors rely on when the enemy is growing stronger. They know that in most cases the enemy within uses pride, fear, jealousy, selfish ambition, complacency, and similar weapons to destroy individuals and communities.

The first time you read this scripture, you might think it's about making ourselves strong to stand up to the attack—putting on the breastplate and helmet, taking up the sword. Look again: "Be strong *in the Lord* and in the strength of *His* might.

Put on the full armor *of God*."

This scripture isn't about our strength. It's about trusting His strength.

It's not about power. It's about trust.

We move further down the road toward great when we stop relying on our own strength and start to trust God and one another.

On Saturday night, halfway through the fourth quarter, Wes Byrum walked down the sideline to Josh Harris and Neil Caudle and told them, "Do whatever you have to do to get your minds right. We're going to drive down and kick a field goal to win it."

Kentucky had just tied the game 34–34 with a touchdown. We had fumbled the ensuing kickoff but recovered it at our own seven-yard line, then started on offense ninety-three yards from the goal line.

Yet Wes trusted the offense.

You can look at a dozen moments in the 2010 season and say all of them were critical to our success, but I believe Saturday night on the road in Lexington, Kentucky, on this fourth-quarter drive from the shadow of our own end zone, our guys made a decision to be great, not just good. They made a conscious decision to believe in one another and to live by faith. To trust.

The offense used seven plays to push the ball to midfield, and Wes told Neil and Josh to get ready. In a close game, a smart kicker knows the score, the time, and how many time-outs each team has so he can prepare himself for what's coming. He knows when to start warming up by kicking balls into a net, and when the moment arrives, he's ready to be perfect.

Sure enough, Kentucky started calling time-outs, hoping to leave enough time on the clock after we scored to get one more chance. During one of those breaks, I stepped away from the sideline to watch Wes practice. In that moment he became a different man. His eyes locked onto something I couldn't see, focused like an animal about to charge its prey. I remember Carnell Williams had that look. Carnell was a running back for Auburn from 2001 to 2004, and when his eyes locked in like that before he ran onto the field, nobody was going to stop him.

Wes had almost lost the opportunity to regain that focus. I mentioned earlier the tough season he experienced as a sophomore in 2008. Well, not long after Coach Chizik and his staff arrived at Auburn in January 2009, Wes got into trouble with his new coaches, and he lost their trust. In response, the coaches enforced a nine o'clock curfew for the remainder of the semester. Every night Wes had to be home. If he needed to go to the library at night, he called an assistant coach, who drove over to the library and checked on him.

Wes didn't have a roommate, so when he wasn't in class or at practice, he walked a lonely road. He did a lot of reading, and he read the Bible more than he ever had. On those long nights at home alone, he recommitted himself to becoming the best he could be. That commitment began with making right decisions as basic as cooking healthy meals for himself. He prepared all his own meals and even his snacks. No junk food.

There comes a time in the life of a Christian when we realize we are not living a life that is worthy of the gospel. In Wes's case, his realization started with something more basic. He had not been living a life worthy of Auburn University football. Then, through the discipline process, his faith grew. He learned to trust something and someone stronger than his right leg.

On that October night in Kentucky, he trusted the offense to get the ball in position for him to kick a field goal to win the game. The offense trusted Wes to make that kick. They drove down to the seven-yard line and called time-out with two seconds left in the game. Wes, Neil, and Josh ran onto the field. Wes made the kick and we won the game.

FEELING GOD'S
PLEASURE

T HERE IS A lightness about Cam Newton. A sweetness,
even. Other players ran onto the field before a football
game, pumped up by the coaches and the crowd, ready for the
first hit. Cam skipped from one end of the stadium to the other
and back again, smiling like an eight-year-old on a playground,
just out there to have fun. Sometimes he held his arms out like
an airplane and "flew" around the field.

Then the game started, and fans wondered if he might actually take off and fly.

Olympic sprinter Eric Liddell, who inspired the movie
Chariots of Fire, said, "I believe God made me for a purpose, but
He also made me fast. And when I run I feel His pleasure."

Cam plays football as if he feels God's pleasure. I've seen him smile when he's running downfield.

God made Cam for a purpose, but He also gave him amazing physical tools for playing football.

Now the game is giving Cam a platform to achieve God's purpose for his life, and I believe he is ready.

Thousands of Auburn kids wear number 2, and they want to be Cam Newton. Then Cam opens his mouth and says, "I thank God every single day. I'm just His instrument, and He's using me on a consistent basis daily."

For those kids, Cam is their hero, and they hear him say that. The greatest athlete on the planet is bragging on Jesus, and young people are watching and listening.

Thirty years ago one of my teammates at Auburn, a deeply committed Christian, ran onto the field at Jordan-Hare Stadium for the first game of his freshman year, and he was almost overwhelmed by the roar of sixty-five thousand people standing and cheering for the Orange and Blue. With his spine tingling and the hair on his arms standing on end, he thought, *This is nothing but a platform for the gospel.* We are far from seeing Todd Burkhalter's vision fulfilled. In fact, some days the football field seems like anything but a platform for the gospel.

But this is what I *have* seen happen in Jordan-Hare and in other stadiums: I have seen grace and healing that overwhelms me. I've seen young men on both sidelines pray together for injured players. I've seen Christ use football as a platform to mend broken relationships and bind up broken hearts. I've even seen Him save lives. In fact, through football, He saved my life. He saved me and set me free to be everything He wants me to be. He can free you too.

He set us all free to live our lives the way Cam Newton plays football. Full speed. Never looking back.

"Forgetting what lies behind," the apostle Paul wrote, "and reaching forward to what lies ahead, I press on toward the goal for the prize of the upward call of God in Christ Jesus."

Do you hear what Paul is saying? "I'm not looking back. This Roman prison I'm writing from won't keep me from reaching my goal. Neither will my own sin."

Paul said he is *reaching* and *pressing* for the goal. I like to think of him as running full speed, sidestepping linebackers and defensive backs, putting his hand down to catch his balance, reading and playing off his blockers, then dragging the final defender across the goal line. If you saw Cam's forty-nine-yard run against LSU, then you know what I'm talking about. He would not be denied the goal line. Neither would Paul, and neither should we. Satan uses our shame and our guilt to prevent us from living the joy Christ offers. But we are forgiven. Christ died so we can live free.

"I had a long journey to get where I am right now," Cam said. "Spiritually, it's been a long process. But I can say to this day that junior college was the best thing that ever happened to me. I found myself. I was young and naive at Florida. I pray every morning, thanking God for putting me in the situation I'm in."

Then Cam added, "He's using me to extend His Word, and

I'm a prime example of how God can turn something that was bad into something that is very great."

Cam wasn't claiming personal greatness. He was saying that he was *declared* great through Christ. That is the gospel! We are declared great through our faith in Christ. And then we can be transformed.

That transformation, Jesus said, should lead us to "become like little children."

Nobody on the team was more childlike than Cam, and nobody loved children more. When we were playing with the children in the Dominican Republic, Cam said, "I was trying to put a smile on the face of every little kid out there, whether it was throwing a baseball, kicking a soccer ball, or shooting hoops. I just wanted to make them smile. We had candy to share, and I had mine for about two minutes. I was giving it out so fast. They brought tears to my eyes to see their smiles."

Cam also knew when to put away childish things. In early August, Cam went to Wrights Mill Elementary School in Auburn and asked the principal if he could mentor kids who might be at risk. For the rest of the year, Cam went to the school every Monday, the only day the players don't have football obligations during the season, and mentored fifth-grade boys, holding them accountable for their grades and their behavior.

Sweetness and light alongside discipline and accountability, and feeling God's pleasure.

THE END
OF ONE ROAD

OCTOBER 18, 2010

AAIRON SAVAGE WAS angry with God. Really angry. And I knew better than to get in the way. The two of them had to work this one out.

On October 16 God allowed the thing Aairon loved most to be taken from him in a career-ending play against Arkansas. He was left alone in the middle of the field with a broken leg while his friend Zac Etheridge ran for a touchdown and cheers echoed across the Plains.

When we see others on their broken road, we're tempted to ease their pain by telling them how God has a good reason for their loss or a bigger plan in mind. That's nothing but spiritual nonsense to the man who feels deserted by his Lord. We're smarter sometimes to keep our mouths shut.

God didn't expect Aairon to thank Him for his broken leg or praise Him for allowing him to suffer. God wants us to pray authentically, not religiously. Yell at Him, if we need to, but be honest. The psalmist didn't hold back:

WHY DO YOU STAND AFAR OFF, O LORD?
WHY DO YOU HIDE YOURSELF
IN TIMES OF TROUBLE?
(10:1, NASB)

I WILL SAY TO GOD MY ROCK,
"WHY HAVE YOU FORGOTTEN ME?"
(42:9, NASB)

AWAKE, LORD! WHY DO YOU SLEEP?
(44:23)

The writer of the Psalms didn't hesitate to tell God, sometimes disrespectfully, that he felt abandoned as the waters rose all around him.

On Monday morning, Aairon was scheduled for surgery at Dr. Andrews' clinic in Pensacola, and I went down to be with him and his family. Driving across the Pensacola Bay Bridge, over three miles of salt water, I rolled down the window and breathed deep the damp, salty air. For a few minutes Aairon drifted out of my mind, and I was a kid again with my dad and my brothers. One weekend every summer, a long time ago, Pop piled us in the car and drove the back roads from our home in Winston, Georgia, through Alabama and west Florida to this very spot to catch fish in the bay. There was an abandoned two-lane bridge that ran alongside the road I was driving on now, and it had been converted into a mile-and-a-half-long fishing pier out to the middle of the bay. Fishermen drove their cars and trucks onto that old bridge and parked along both sides to fish.

In the days leading up to our annual trip, I went to bed every night wondering if we'd catch an ugly puffer fish or an eel or some other bizarre creature. Fishing in salt water wasn't like back home, where we knew what we'd catch: catfish or bream or bass. Down here, when our line tugged there was no telling what we'd pull in. We might even get a stingray or a small shark.

Our adventure always started long before daylight on a summer Saturday morning. Mama woke us up with the smell of bacon, and my brothers staggered out of bed. But I jumped out and dressed as fast as I could so we could leave quickly.

We ate and then went out in the dark and climbed into the car, and Pop drove out to the interstate that ran right behind our house. He turned south, and we rode in silence for a couple of hours until the sun rose over the Alabama pine trees. Then sometime around nine in the morning, he pulled into the parking lot of a little bait shop at the edge of the bay and bought some shrimp for bait and some ice for the cooler. We got sardines and cheese crackers and peanuts and Cokes for lunch, then Pop drove us slowly out onto the old bridge. He drove and drove and drove past fishermen leaning on the old concrete sides. The bridge finally ran out, and we got out of the car. I put a shrimp on my hook and threw it off the end into the bay, then sat on a bucket. I waited for the fish, and I looked across the water and wondered what the fishermen in the boats out there might be catching.

We fished all day and caught sea trout and flounder and other fish I didn't know, but the fishermen close by said they were good eating, so Pop cleaned them and threw them into the cooler. The sun went down over the bay, and a dozen lanterns down the bridge hissed and burned so bright I could hardly look at them. Clouds of gnats swarmed around the lights, so nobody stood right beside them. They cranked up camp stoves on metal tables, and before long the smells of hot oil and fried fish made me hungry. We were saving our fish for Sunday night, so we bought our supper from a man selling snacks from the back of his truck. I sat on my bucket and looked up at the stars until I got sleepy and went back to the car.

We all took turns sleeping and fishing throughout the night. Then, sometime after sunrise on Sunday, we started home with a cooler filled to the top with fish, knowing everybody was waiting for us back in Winston, where Pop would fry up everything we'd caught and feed all of our friends.

I'm sure that when I was a boy fishing on the old bridge, I never thought of Peter and Andrew or the sons of Zebedee dropping their nets to follow Jesus. And when we got back home and opened the cooler to show Mama our dozens of beautiful fish packed on ice, I was not reminded of the apostles' nets bursting with fish the Master had provided.

Now, I drove across the water toward Dr. Andrews' clinic to

be with Aairon in his surgery, and all those thoughts washed over me and seeped into my boyhood memories. Jesus did powerful work and performed many miracles on and around the water. Now here was Aairon, standing on the end of the bridge—the end of his football career—looking out across the water.

What miracle did God have in mind?

IGNITE!

NOVEMBER 11, 2010

WE PRAYED FOR a revival on campus—a revival of the Holy Spirit.

In March, Will Graham, grandson of evangelist Billy Graham, had brought a weekend crusade to Auburn and attracted nearly twenty thousand people from across east Alabama and west Georgia. We believed our students needed an event of their own, so we scheduled *Ignite!* for November 4, which was the Thursday night of homecoming week, in the brand-new Auburn Arena.

Jay Jacobs and Coach Chizik supported us at every step. Jay agreed to open the evening with a prayer, and Gene offered to speak. I did not take their commitments lightly. As athletic director and head football coach, Jay and Gene were incredibly busy during football season. Yet they both wanted to take advantage of opportunities to share the gospel in our community. For Gene, those opportunities came primarily during the off-season. On Thursday evenings during the season, he had his *Tiger Talk* radio show, and he was otherwise totally focused on his players and our next opponent. He would be taking time away from preparations less than forty-eight hours before kickoff.

The team was undefeated after nine games, and Cam Newton was considered by many to be the leading candidate for the Heisman Trophy. That success multiplied Gene's media demands.

Then, late on Thursday afternoon, just before *Ignite!* was scheduled to begin, ESPN reported serious allegations regarding Cam's recruitment coming out of junior college. This was another huge distraction for both Gene and Jay, and under the circumstances it would have been perfectly understandable for them to have passed on *Ignite!*

I don't believe that possibility crossed either man's mind. Instead, Jay arrived early and prayed with us for the students who would be arriving soon. By that time, Gene was already on his radio show in front of an audience at the Ariccia Restaurant across campus at the Hotel at Auburn University.

The lights went down, and Jay stepped onstage to welcome thousands of students to the new arena. Then he prayed, "Heavenly Father, we are in awe of Your presence and the blessings You have poured out on us. We know that being Christians doesn't prevent us from going through tough times. But we know that when we do, You are there holding us. You are holding our hand, carrying us through those tough times. So as students and others go through tough times and relationships and school and family, we know You have us. Thank You for that blessing . . ."

If I didn't know Jay's heart for reaching young people with the hope of Christ, I might have thought he was praying for himself and the trials he was anticipating for the entire athletic department.

After I spoke and told some of my own story, Gene arrived and came onstage. And on a night when the whole sports world seemed to be talking about Auburn football in a negative way, here's what Coach Gene Chizik had to say to Auburn students at *Ignite!*:

This is the first time in a long time that I get to go to a place where people choose to talk about something other than Auburn football. I take this very seriously. And the first thing I would say to you tonight is you are not here by mistake. You are all here for a reason. A girlfriend or boyfriend might have brought you, or you might have seen the crowd and walked in with them to check it out. But you were supposed to be here tonight. However you got here, that's how God works.

I told our team last week how hard it is for you to believe, in this day and age, unless you see it or touch it or feel it or experience it; how hard it is for you to believe that a man two thousand years ago walked on earth. And I'm supposed to hang everything I've got on Him and the fact that this guy came to earth and was sent by God to die on the cross for me for my sins? Because I can't see Him, I can't touch Him, and I can't feel Him. Is this real?

In this day and age, you are so into technology, that's a little challenging for you. I was brought up going to church and being told this is the way we were going to do it. At that point in my life I don't know if I understood and valued what it meant to bring God into my life. To have a relationship that is so strong.

Right now, every day, when I address my football team with 125 guys in the room, some of those guys never knew who their mom was. Some never knew who their dad was. Some have parents who are alcoholics or drug addicts or crack addicts. And those things apply to many of you at some point.

Everybody here at some point along the line has experienced that or knows somebody who has. That stuff is real. It's out there. I look at these guys and you guys and know that you live in such a tough world. You're going to walk out of here tonight, and your friend is going to do something tonight. And you decided, instead, to be here.

Well, let me give you this message. I promise you I'm not standing up here with a halo on my head. The first thing I did when I realized I didn't have the relationship with Christ that I really needed was to get on my knees. I submitted to God that I am truly sorry. I'm weak and I'm a wretch, in this world right now, and there is no way I can live and be strong without You in my life.

It's a lonely feeling when you think you have to deal with that by yourself. You don't. I told my team two weeks ago on Friday night, "You're looking at a weak man. The only difference between me and some other guy is that I know I'm weak, and I get down on my knees every night. And before my feet hit the floor in the morning, I thank God for waking me up, and I ask Him to give me strength, because I am weak."

So whenever you think I look strong, it's not me. When people ask, "How do you deal with all that?" it's not me. When they say, "You've got all this going on," it's not me. There is no way I would be bold enough to take credit for anything that's happened in my life and say, "It's Gene Chizik." Everything that has happened to me, my steps have been ordered. I just try to submit.

I have a beautiful family, a beautiful wife, and three beautiful children. I have a job that requires so many hours of my time every day that I cannot be a good husband, I cannot be a good father, I cannot be a good football coach if I'm relying on Gene Chizik. I can't do it. I don't want to do it.

If I'm ever walking around with my chest out like nothing can faze me, there's one reason. I believe God has got my back.

Maybe some of you guys are afraid because you want to go in the right direction, but you don't want to give up this or doing that. God knows that you are weak. God knows you can't do it. That's why you pray. That's why you read the Word.

That's why you dig into that stuff, because that's how you get stronger. Do you think you can go in the weight room one time in four months and get stronger? You're not going to do that. Do you think you can go to an aerobics class once in four months and stay in shape? No, you have to keep working at it.

When I started coaching. I just wanted to win. All I was going to do was win. But as God started changing my life, He started telling me, "This winning thing, you keep doing it, but what you really need to be doing is changing the lives of eighteen- to twenty-two-year-olds you're around every day." I started thinking that maybe this whole thing isn't about just winning.

God says, "I just want you to trust Me."

In 2004 when I was here with Brother Chette, we had a very spiritual group of players. They wore T-shirts with Proverbs 3:5–6 printed on them:

TRUST IN THE LORD WITH ALL YOUR HEART
AND LEAN NOT ON YOUR OWN UNDERSTANDING;
IN ALL YOUR WAYS ACKNOWLEDGE HIM,
AND HE WILL MAKE YOUR PATHS STRAIGHT.

That's hard to do when things are not looking good. But know He will never forsake you. He will never leave you. Trusting God is a life-changing proposition.

Make sure you know that when you walk out the door, the devil will be waiting on you. When you go back to your dorm, he's waiting on you. At the sorority house, he's waiting on you. Are you strong enough to say no? If you are not, the devil will say you're a coward, and he's going to smile.

I encourage you tonight to grab somebody you think is leaning toward accepting Jesus Christ. Don't be afraid to talk about it. Don't be afraid to talk about what you are.

And if you want to walk around courageous, if you want to walk around confident, the only way I know to do that is to pray, "God pick me up, give me Your wisdom, and carry me."

If you're willing to submit and say that, He will change your life.

You never know what's going to happen the next minute of your life. We're at practice, in meetings, in class, in games. Prayer time is the one night we have to open up and let our teammates know how we feel on the inside. Not many teams can do that, because guys are afraid of what the next guy's going to think. But those times held us together as one family.

ANTOINE CARTER

FAMILY STRENGTH

THE DAY BEFORE the biggest game of the season, we gathered as a family to celebrate Thanksgiving and to earnestly thank God for His blessings. You might think of a better place than the indoor practice facility for a holiday meal, but the "field" was perfect for us. The coaches' wives and children were all there. Lakeba and our children were there. And a lot of players' parents and siblings joined us for a joyous occasion and tons of food. Then at four o'clock, after we had finished dinner, the players, staff, and I went out to the buses and began our journey to Tuscaloosa. A few hours later we were in our circle praying.

When you roll into another team's stadium, you want to make a statement early in the game. Push them around on either side of the ball, and you can rattle their confidence. That didn't happen for us against Alabama. They scored a touchdown the first time they got the ball. And the second. And the third. Early in the second quarter they led 21–0 and were driving for a fourth touchdown. They must have thought they had rattled our confidence and were ready to put their foot on our throat. In fact, some of our guys were shaken. They had missed assignments and missed tackles.

Offensive tackle Lee Ziemba remembered the night in Baton Rouge over a year earlier when Coach Jeff Grimes had told his players, "It takes a man to play hard when you're down by twenty-eight. Now go out there and play!" So Ziemba refused to look at the scoreboard, instead thinking only about the next series and the next play.

Defensive end Antoine Carter says nobody on the team was looking to blame anybody else. "That was the main thing that helped us win all season," Antoine says. "Everybody was working together, and when things went wrong, nobody was pointing a finger. Instead, we leaned on each other. Then we went on to the next play.

"Coach Chizik talked about family from the beginning, and we really came together. There were no black or white groups. No offense and defense groups. Everybody just hung together. There wasn't any separation anywhere on the team. Nothing divided us."

Not even a three-touchdown deficit only thirteen minutes into the Alabama game.

Antoine looks back on his play that changed the momentum of the game and says, "In the big picture, it tells me not to quit on anything I do. You never know what's going to happen. That play opened my eyes a lot more than anything else I had ever experienced about never giving up."

The play had begun at the Alabama forty-yard line with Antoine lined up at left defensive end. The Alabama quarterback dropped back to pass, and Antoine fought against the Alabama right tackle. They were eight yards behind the line of scrimmage when the quarterback released the ball, and Antoine immediately turned and chased. Running back Mark Ingram caught the ball at the forty and turned to run. In that split second Antoine picked up two yards on Ingram. Eltoro Freeman got an arm on Ingram, and Antoine gained another yard. Then Ingram raced toward the goal line, sixty yards away, and his speed was too much for Antoine. Seven Auburn defenders stood in Ingram's way, and Antoine might have relied on one of them to stop him, but he chose to keep chasing. Each time Ingram dodged a man, Antoine gained a step. Then Zac Etheridge hit Ingram near the sideline at the twenty-yard line, causing him to stumble. Antoine closed the final three-yard gap, catching him from behind with his left arm and reaching around with his right to punch the ball as hard as he could. It was a drill the defense practiced every day, and he knocked the ball out of Ingram's arms. The ball bounced down the sideline all the way into the end zone, where Demond Washington recovered it for us. Instead of being behind 28–0, we had hope, because Antoine Carter had chosen not to stop.

They had sung "Lean on Me" over and over throughout the season, and each week another guy stepped up to be the rock. Over the next three quarters, Nick Fairley and Cam Newton, Terrell Zachery and Emory Blake, Philip Lutzenkirchen and Neiko Thorpe, Josh Bynes and T'Sharvan Bell, and twenty other guys would all take a turn as the rock, because that's what it would take for them to deliver one of the greatest wins in Auburn history. They all leaned on each other when they were trailing 24–0 in Bryant-Denny Stadium, and they walked out undefeated and closer as a family than ever.

CURSE
OF PROSPERITY

BEFORE HIS DOWNFALL A MAN'S HEART IS PROUD.
PROVERBS 18:12 (HCSB)

T HE VERY THING we wished for might have become our stumbling block. We were 12–0 and preparing to play for the Southeastern Conference championship, and for the first time all season the demons that accompany prosperity—pride, envy, entitlement, selfishness—found their way into the locker room. It was a minor issue, but one that could have become major if we ignored it. Earlier in the week some of the younger players were bothered that the SEC Championship game tickets they received for their families were not as good as the tickets upperclassmen were given. They didn't make a big deal about it, just some conversations among themselves, like, "I've worked just as hard as he has. I can't believe he got this or that and I didn't.'"

But it was the only opening Satan needed to slip in and begin his work.

He turns our small stumble into his opportunity, and he magnifies any situation, puts some heat on it, and stirs the pot to get it smoking.

A good coaching staff stays close enough to the players to know whenever divisive issues pop up, and they weren't taking any chances with this one. On Tuesday I had asked Trooper Taylor to speak at our chapel the night before the championship game, and he decided to hit the ticket issue head-on by speaking directly to the bigger concern: the distractions of ego and envy.

So many alumni and students were telling the players how great they were—especially after the Alabama win—our guys were tempted to start believing them. It's a natural response, and Trooper knew that.

"All season you've been looking out for each other," Trooper said, "and you were not so concerned about yourselves. You surrendered your personal desires for the team. You've had all kinds of outside distractions, but you stayed focused on what was out there in front of you. You focused on the goal at hand, and you made sure you gave God the glory.

"Now a lot of people are patting us on the back," he continued, "and it's easy to get distracted. It's easy to start thinking we're special and deserve something special. Well, you ask Cam about junior college, where you carry your own shoulder pads when you walk to the bus. Ask him what *special* is. You guys fly on planes to games, stay in nice hotels, and you can eat as much food as you want. And you want to complain about tickets? In the Bible, when the people had it as good as you do and they started complaining, God found a way to wipe those folks out and start over again.

"You need to start thanking God for your blessings, because what God gives, He can take away. Don't go taking His blessings for granted."

It was a strong message, and Trooper wasn't letting anybody off the hook. He told the story of the apostle Peter getting out of the boat to walk on the water to Jesus. "As long as Peter kept his eyes on the prize," Trooper said, "as long as he kept looking at Jesus, he was fine. But as soon as he started looking at the waves around him and thinking about the storm out there, he started sinking. That's what will happen to you if you let these little issues distract you."

Then he started reminding them of a few blessings we had experienced throughout the year, both on the field and off, and he reminded us that God inspires a lot of our "coincidences."

A couple of weeks earlier, for example, Trooper had missed Friday night chapel because he was on a recruiting trip at a high school football game. Driving home on the interstate, he narrowly missed colliding with a truck that swerved toward him and forced him to veer toward another truck.

"I still don't know how I made it through," he said, "other than God was with me, because there's no way I should have missed those trucks on the interstate. I'm not that good a driver, and I know those guys in those eighteen-wheelers weren't that good a driver, either. That was a miracle."

Later he was kneeling at the altar of his church when the associate pastor's wife came over and quietly told him she and other women in the church were continuing to pray for our players. She named several injured players on her list and asked if they should add anyone else. Trooper asked her to pray for another player, and at that moment his phone buzzed. That same player was texting Trooper, asking him to pray for him. It was a little thing, Trooper said—maybe a coincidence—but when your focus is on God and His blessings, each of these situations can uplift.

"We wait around sometimes," he said, "for God to give us big miracles like changing water into wine or raising somebody from the dead. Zac Etheridge is a living testimony to God's miracles. But we experience God's miracles every day, miracles that aren't so public. It's a miracle for us just to open our eyes in the morning."

Then he brought the message to blessings on the field. "I never tell anybody that God keeps score," he said, "but I do believe God puts us on a platform where we can share His message, and our responsibility is to remember that He gave us an opportunity as a team and as a Christian family. You take a ball that's getting punched out from a running back who never fumbles, and the ball stays six inches from the sidelines and rolls out the back of the end zone. I've been around football seventeen years, and I've never seen a football roll so straight so far like that. I'm not saying God kept it in, but I am saying that because it stayed in, we have an opportunity and a responsibility that we wouldn't have had otherwise. And the message we send cannot be one of bickering."

Then Trooper closed with a final reminder of God's greatest blessing. "What a football player does," he said, "is all about performance. If players don't perform, they don't play.

"Who a football player is, however, is about grace. God is going to bless you and love you, and He's not going to love you in slices. He's not going to take you just when you're scoring touchdowns or when life is good. God already loves you. God always loves you.

"It doesn't matter whether you score a hundred touchdowns or even find a cure for cancer, God loves you and He's paid the price for your salvation by sending His only Son to die for you. So what else can you do? Your job now is to give God the glory, and the rest will take care of itself."

With that, the players broke into position meetings with their coaches before coming back together for our prayer meeting later in the evening, and almost every player on the team came to pray. Trooper had set the stage for a special time together.

"I look at Friday night as the glue that held this team together," he says. "It's the only time the teammates get a chance to hear about each other's problems that they normally would not know. These kids don't all have the same interests—one kid might be interested in country music and come from a totally different background from another kid who listens to rap music and goes to a different club. But on Friday night, when we sit in that circle together, they get to hear about each other's problems at home and with their families. One kid looks at another and he doesn't have any idea that the other one has problems at home. He thinks the other guy is from a well-to-do family, and he has no idea that his mother is sick and dying. We hear about that in the prayer meeting, and we ask each other to pray for us."

By the end of the evening the players had put away any distractions that had divided them, and once again we were one body in Christ.

I admire so many guys on this team because of how they live their life day in and day out, on and off the field. Their war is for the Lord. Guys like Aairon Savage and Zac Etheridge. People look up to them. To see their model daily keeps me motivated and on my toes spiritually. Neil Caudle and Kodi Burns. We can talk about our faith with all of these guys. They are leaders. To be a leader you must be a good follower, and I follow those guys who have a good grasp of the Word.

CAM NEWTON

ONE MORE ROAD

NEIL CAUDLE THINKS God must have sense of humor. For five seasons Neil stood on the sidelines as a backup quarterback, signaling plays from the coaches to the huddle, all the time longing to be on the field for every down. "Then on the last play of my Auburn career," Neil says, "the last football play ever in my life, God showed me where I needed to be."

With the score tied 19–19 and two seconds left in the national championship game, Neil took the snap, placed the ball, and held it for Wes Byrum to kick the winning field goal.

Neil had said before the game that if he had his way, the outcome would be decided on a final kick, with him holding the ball for Wes to win.

Wes had similar thoughts. "You dream as a little kid to make the kick to win a championship. Then the time comes when we're about to complete the journey, and there's nothing anybody can do to take it away from us. It was an overwhelming feeling of confidence and excitement."

Just like in their dreams, Coach Chizik called time-out with two seconds left and the ball on the two-yard line. The kicking team ran onto the field and did their job. Josh made the snap, Neil held the ball, leaning it forward and a little to the right, the way Wes likes it, and Wes made the kick.

David Housel, Auburn athletic director emeritus, said in his unique way what so many Auburn people were thinking: "It pleases me to no end that the last Auburn hand—the last piece of Auburn flesh and blood to touch that football before it went through the uprights—was Neil Caudle's. He represents all that Auburn football is and should be, all the way back to Coach Dye, Coach Jordan, and in particular, George Petrie. If you look down through the years of an Auburn football player in victory, in defeat, in joy, in sadness, and the stick-to-itiveness of what Auburn at its best is intended to be, it all comes together in men like Neil Caudle."

Neil had been where God wanted him all along the way, leading by example at practice, in the locker room, in the prayer room, on campus, and in the community.

Kodi Burns, the other team leader who had been passed over as a starting quarterback, also found himself in the spotlight in the championship game. Early in the second quarter Kodi scored the first touchdown of the game, his first touchdown of the season. It was as if the coaches had designed a play to honor Kodi for the sacrifice he had made and the price he had paid for his university. Cam Newton passed to Kodi at the twenty-yard line, and Kodi sidestepped and outran the Oregon safeties to the goal line.

After the game Neil and Kodi and twenty-one other seniors lifted off their shoulder pads for the last time as Auburn football players. For some, the familiar lightness they felt when they stepped out of their uniforms gave way to a moment of lostness as they wondered where the next road would begin, and where it would lead. In the midst of their celebration of a national championship, a piece of them was dying. An identity that had defined them since they were little boys would exist only in memory, and they were stepping into the reality that football is what they do, it is not who they are. Once they realize that, there is a sense of freedom for the athlete. Without it, they are in bondage to the sport.

Their teammate Aairon Savage, whose career had ended with his injury in the Arkansas game, had returned to the sidelines to serve as a powerful model, accepting with grace the inevitability that each of them now faced.

For the rest of their lives these Auburn football players will talk about the 2010 national championship season—and not just the football. In February 2011, a month after the national championship game, the Montgomery Quarterback Club presented its Player of the Year award to Ryan Pugh. Lee Ziemba surprised the crowd by joining Ryan at the event, and the two friends stood at the microphone and discussed the season, the championship, and their four years together on the offensive line at Auburn. But not for long. For Lee and Ryan, there is more than one definition of *glory days*. They changed the subject from football to Antonia, the woman they had met in the Dominican Republic. They described for their audience her broken house, the broken village of Aguas Negras, and the children living at the trash dump. They talked about what being thirsty means when there is no clean water to drink, and what hunger is like for a child who might have to bargain for his next meal. They recalled their pleasure playing with the laughing children and worshiping with the Dominican villagers.

They tried to explain the difference between the momentary happiness they experienced on Saturdays—their mountaintops, where they didn't even have to squeeze their own water bottles—and the abiding joy of walking through the valley every day on a long, broken road with their teammates.

• • •

Three months later, on a sunny spring morning, more than three thousand Auburn students marched onto Pat Dye Field in Jordan-Hare Stadium in their caps and gowns, with their families in the stands applauding politely. It was a warm day for the graduates in their black, and the reading of all those names went slowly.

Then they heard the name, "Kodi Burns," and the students, almost by instinct, rose to their feet and cheered their classmate.

Kodi Burns! They had arrived at Auburn together with Kodi fresh out of high school in the fall of 2007, and had watched him burst onto the scene on this same field as the future of the football program. Kodi had represented their own promise, their potential. Then his disappointments on the field mirrored their own private setbacks as they grew together into young adults. His broken road was theirs. His touchdown in the national championship game was their hope.

They heard Kodi's name called, and they stood in respect as he walked across the stage to receive his diploma. He was one of them, and he was a hero to them. Not the kind of hero they anticipated when they first saw him run with a football, but the kind of hero they wanted to be and could be. The kind of hero that is tested and proven on a broken road.

Like Kodi, and like those three thousand graduates, we reach the end of the road and realize we are not who we thought we were. But we are becoming who God wants us to be.

Then there is another road.

TO THE HEART
OF GOD

SOMETIMES EVERY ROAD leads into the desert. You taste the dust with every step and try to remember when and why the living got this hard. You look around for your friends and realize you are alone.

Weren't they just here? When did they turn back? Or was it you who turned?

On a Saturday night in June 2012, I was in Birmingham for a speaking engagement. Reggie and Michelle Torbor had invited me to stay the night in their home, and Reggie and I watched the Heat and the Celtics in the final game of the NBA championship. I had just called Lakeba to tell her good night and was getting ready for bed when my cell phone rang. It was Gene Chizik. He spoke low, pain evident in his voice. There was a tragedy in Auburn. Three young men were dead—two of them had been our players. He said the players' names, and it felt like my heart was pierced. Ed and Ladarious (we called him Da Da, pronounced "Dae Dae").

My mind instantly went to the quiet lake behind our house. Sometimes in the late afternoon when I drove home from campus, Da Da would be standing on the bank fishing. I'd get out of my truck and holler down at him, "What you got?" He would smile and lift up a big catfish.

"You gonna cook that thing?" I'd ask.

"Yes sir," he'd call back.

He might fish until dark, then take his catch home and fry them up for friends.

Then I thought of Ed. Such a big man—six feet six, and he must have weighed three hundred fifty pounds. He would sit on the sofa in my office visiting, and whenever anybody else came in, he would stand up and fill the room. I know it's a cliché, but it seems the biggest players are often the quietest. Ed was one of the big guys, and he was like a giant teddy bear. We prayed together many, many times after the doctor told him he couldn't play anymore because of a back injury. He had found peace in his loss and was staying in school to earn his degree.

"Do you want me to call their parents?" I asked Gene.

"No," he said. "I'll call."

A lot of coaches talk about their commitment to their players as a father-son relationship. Gene lived that commitment, even after players were no longer on the team. When the families and friends traveled to Auburn to mourn their loss at a student-led candlelight vigil, Gene spent time with them, accompanied them to the vigil, then stayed with them into the night in a quiet room at the Athletic Complex, offering what comfort he could.

Some people believe that where Christ is, there is no suffering. That is not true. The truth is, where there is suffering, there is Christ. Gene, by his actions and words, offered Christ's comfort.

There were times in 2012 when Gene was more of a chaplain than I was, with a stronger ministry to players and coaches than mine. His own road and that of the team had led into the desert, and for twelve Saturdays the world watched and speculated and questioned. Throughout the season, Gene never doubted God's love or His presence, even in the worst of times. Not when his mother died in October. Not when he lost his job in December. He let us witness his faith, and that faith convinced us that God's promises really are true—promises of hope and peace beyond our ability to understand, and a promise that nothing we encounter on this broken road will separate us from His love.

• • •

Two roads. One led to crystal, the other to dust. Yet both roads lead us to the very place we seek: the heart of God. Because when we journey with God and accept the challenges and risks of the broken road, we are pilgrims on our way to a holy place, no matter what we encounter along the way.

I am reminded of a story about two brokenhearted men walking down the road soon after Jesus was crucified. The risen

Christ joined them, but they didn't realize who He was until after He had left.

Then they asked each other, "Were not our hearts burning within us while He was speaking to us on the road?"

That's the way it is when we walk with Him.

Now another road rises to meet us and transform us, and He waits there to walk with us, encourage us, strengthen us, and share His peace. Wherever that road leads.

scope of the present study. The fourth skirmish noted in this passage took place at Gath, and the highlight of the action was the killing by David's nephew Jonathan of another of the Rephaite champions who had six fingers on each hand and six toes on each foot.

C. David's Song (22:1-51)

During the latter part of David's reign, after his reestablishment on the throne and perhaps with the realization that he would go out to war no more (21:17), he composed this psalm of thankgiving for victory over all his enemies. The psalm itself claims to be of Davidic authorship. Jewish tradition supports that assertion, and modern critics are almost unanimous in attributing it to him. The text is essentially the same as that of Psalm 18, but dozens of minor divergences occur in the two recensions. Some critics attribute them to the carelessness of scribes in copying the text, but the differences are not the type that normally would occur for that reason. Many scholars believe that David wrote both, that the Samuel text is the original, and that David altered it slightly for liturgical purposes when it became part of the Psalms. Others believe that neither is the original but that David altered the original for use in the Psalms, and the sacred historian made minor changes for incorporation into this historical work. In any case the message is essentially the same in both works.

The sacred historian clearly indicates that the psalm is intended to celebrate David's deliverance from Saul and a variety of other enemies (v. 1). After an introduction (vv. 2-4), David evidently depicted deliverance from Saul's presecution under the figure of a remarkable divine appearance (vv. 5-20), sought to explain the ground of his deliverance (vv. 21-28), went on to give thanks for victories over foreign enemies (vv. 29-46), and closed with another paean of praise to God for all His deeds (vv. 47-51).

In the introduction appears the sum and substance of the entire psalm. David heaps up images to convey his confidence of security in God, who is his Defender, Refuge, and Deliverer. The two verbs in verse 4 are in the imperfect and indicate continued action: "I continually call" and "am continually saved." What God had done in the past, He would assuredly do in the present and future. David's experience as a fugitive in the wilds colored his figures of speech both in the introduction and throughout the rest of the psalm. The almost inaccessible rocks and ravines of Palestine offered protection to the harried fugitive, but he placed his real hope in the God whom the geological formations seemed to typify. God was his true fortress, an impregnable place in whom he could hide; and He, like the immovable rock, was characterized by unchangeable faithfulness. Like a shield of the warrior, He protected, and like a horn of a fierce animal, He defended the righteous.

David had often been in danger of death. Its destructive force like agitated billows crashed on rocks along the shore and threatened to overwhelm. Or like the hunter it stalked its prey and caught it in a net ("the cords of the grave coiled around me," v. 6 NIV). In anguish of heart in his desperate plight, he cried to "my God" (v. 7), one to whom he was joined in covenant relation and to whom he belonged. And God in His grace heard from "his temple," His heavenly dwelling place.

And how God answered! The sovereign God of the universe rode forth to battle on behalf of his beleaguered one. He proclaimed His wrath. "Glowing coals and searing heat" (v. 9 NEB), the fire of His divine presence, consumed all that confronted Him. "He bowed the heavens . . . and came down" (v. 10 NASB); the heavens seemed to sink down as Yahweh came riding on the storm clouds. He mounted the cherubim, a winged lion-creature, and seemed to swoop like a vulture toward its prey. Bright arrows of lightning darted from His presence and claps of thunder bespoke His displeasure. He threw His enemies into confusion. The waters that threatened to engulf the psalmist retreated before the presence of God. "He drew me out of deep waters" (v. 17 NIV; the verb is the basis for the name *Moses*, meaning "drawing out"). As Moses was pulled out of the waters of the Nile, so David was rescued from the waters of tribulation. From a narrow defile Yahweh brought him into a wide open area, "a spacious place," because God delighted in him. What an absolutely mind-boggling description of God's intervention on behalf of His servant. Of course, God did not actually employ natural phenomena in this way to rescue David. But He evidently so intervened on various occasions to protect him or give him the victory that David could practically describe God's interpositions in this majestic fashion.

Next is introduced the reason or ground of God's deliverance. It would be easy to conclude on the basis of verses 21–28 that if one does good, God is bound to do good in return—and especially to rescue from harm. But a study of a larger body of Scripture produces quite a different thought. A believer who opposes God and tramples on His law, so to speak, is not in fellowship with God and cannot expect His blessing. Conversely, the one who obeys God and is in fellowship with Him enjoys a relationship in which God is free to bless the individual. He may deliver such a person from harm, but it may not be according to His purpose to do so (thus there have been martyrs down through the ages). If God does not rescue a person from harm, at least He will stand with him in the hour of trial. David was in a right relationship with God, and God rescued him from his enemies; for this David gave thanks.

David spoke of being rewarded according to his "righteousness," according to the "cleanness" of his hands (v. 21). It should not be thought that he was claiming perfect holiness before God. Rather, he was characterized by integrity of character; and his hands were clean because he had not raised them to shed the blood of Saul, God's anointed. He had "kept the ways of the LORD" (v. 22); he had not allowed his anger and frustration to cloud his judgment concerning the law of God and thus to trample it underfoot. Moreover, "all His ordinances were before me" (v. 23); he had studied and meditated on them (cf. Ps. 1:2). This passage indicates that David had a copy of at least part of the Old Testament with him during his desert wanderings and read it or had the help of Abiathar the priest in his efforts to know God and His will more fully through His recorded word.

David was "upright" (v. 24 KJV; or "blameless") before God; he sought to please God in his public and private life. To the "kind" (v. 26 NASB; "merciful," KJV), "blameless," and "pure" (v. 27), God reciprocates in like fashion. But the "haughty" (v. 28) or godless of David's enemies He would bring down in defeat. Presumably the allusion to David's righteousness in this passage refers primarily to his early life and wilderness wanderings; his later life with its sins of adultery and murder do not seem to be in view. Victories over foreign enemies, in the context of which those sins occurred, figure in the following section (vv. 29–46).

As David faced his many enemies, God "made his darkness light" (v. 29), lifted him out of a condition of weakness and depression, and caused the light of His salvation or victory to shine on him. "By your help I can run through a troop" (v.30), break through an enemy formation, and "leap over a wall," scale the walls of heavily fortified cities. "The word of Yahweh is tried" (v. 31) or tested and proved as by fire; thus the truth of His promises is demonstrated. "He is a shield" (v. 31), a sure protection; and He alone is a "rock" (v. 32), a ground of firm confidence. "He makes my feet like those of the gazelle" (v. 34), swift to move over difficult terrain in pursuit of the enemy and in domination of almost inaccessible places.

You give strength so that "my arms can bend a bow of bronze" (v. 35 NIV) and thus display military prowess. "The shield of . . . salvation" (v. 36) is the shield of almighty defense that consists of salvation. "You have broadened my path" (v. 38), have given more room to walk by removing obstructions, and have given uninterrupted victory and strength for combat (v. 40). The completeness of victory is indicated by the act of placing the foot on the neck of prostrate or kneeling prisoners (v. 41) and by the metaphorical language used to describe the vanquished foe (v. 43). Pulverizing them to dust in some cases was literal as bodies left unburied on the battlefield quickly decomposed and crumbled to dust. The enemies of Israel got no help from their idols and not even from praying to Yahweh, because they had no claim to His protection (v. 42).

God also delivered David from the "contentions" (v. 44 NASB; "strife" RSV) of his people, i.e., from internal struggles connected with Ish-Bosheth, Absalom, Sheba, and others. And this deliverance proved to be a natural prelude to supremacy over neighboring powers. One cannot effectively expand from a weak and divided national base. Soon David was able to dominate adjoining nations. Foreigners came "cringing" (v. 45) to him in involuntary homage. Some on the mere rumor of David's victories offered to submit themselves. Foreign peoples "lose heart" (v. 46), despair of being able to resist the victorious David.

In conclusion, David returned to praise of the Lord who had done so much for him (vv. 47-51). In contrast to the gods of the heathen that do not exist and cannot protect their worshipers, or that may have been viewed as dying and rising with the rhythm of the seasons, David could say of his God, "Yahweh lives" (v. 47), for He is the living and saving God. Moreover, He is "the rock of my salvation" (v. 47), the sure unchangeable Savior. He is the One who "avenges" (v. 48; "vengeance in mine," Deut. 32:35, 41; Rom. 12:19); therefore it was not necessary for David to raise his hand against Saul. And He is the One who subjected the adjoining nations to David. So David rendered profound thanks for deliverance and for the prospective blessings promised in the Davidic covenant (2 Sam. 7) to "his descendants forever" (22:51; cf. Ps. 89:19-29).

D. The Last Words of David (23:1-7)

In what sense these are to be considered the "last words" (v. 1) of David is debated. Almost certainly they were not the last words he ever uttered (for example, these probably came before his charge to Solomon in 1 Kings 2:1-9). Some believe them to be his last utterance as an inspired writer. Or possibly they are to be viewed as his last words in the sense of a prophetic utterance or testament somewhat analogous to the prophetic utterances of Jacob (Gen. 49) and Moses (Deut. 33).

The sacred historian refers to David in terms of his lowly origin as son of Jesse, his exaltation to sovereign power and glory as ruler of his people and of the nations, his choice to be king by the special appointment of God (as preeminently the anointed of God he was a type of Christ), and his contributions as sweet singer of Israel (and thus providing spiritual edification for the people of God). In the latter connection he was a musician of some skill (1 Sam. 16:14-23), a composer of laments (2 Sam. 1:17-27; 3:33-34), a writer of psalms (seventy-three of the one hundred fifty canonical psalms bear titles asserting Davidic authorship and others probably were his), and an organizer of the temple worship and song (1 Chron. 15-16; 6:31; 25:1).

After the historian's introduction of David, the king himself made a specific claim to inspiration: "The Spirit of Yahweh spoke in me; his word was on my tongue" (23:2). By inward impression or audible voice the exact words of God were communicated. What follows is to be considered a messianic passage. The Hebrew is difficult and somewhat elliptical. Verse 3 teaches that there will be a Ruler over mankind or the human race who will rule in righteousness or with justice, and He will exercise His authority in the spirit or fear of God. Messiah's rule will be like the light of the rising sun on a cloudless morning. He will bring new life, spiritual and natural, as the warm sun on a Palestinian hillside in a very brief time (hours or days) stimulates the growth of flowers and grasses after a spring rain. Next David throws in a parenthetical statement to the effect that neither he nor his family had had that kind of influence on Israel or mankind—fraught with crime and calamity as his household was.

But God's covenant with him was everlasting and "confirmed in all ways and sure" (23:5; cf. 2 Sam. 7). That is, the covenant itself had built-in indications of failure in David and his line that would not stand in the way of its ultimate fulfillment (cf. 2 Sam. 7:14–15). The last part of 23:5 asks, in effect, "Will He not bring to pass the salvation or preservation promised to him and his house? Will He not grant his desire for the fulfillment of the covenant? And will He not then make his house to grow?"

The righteous or spiritual aspect of Messiah's rule is highlighted in verses 6 and 7. The ungodly are compared to thorns that men root out and burn to clear the ground of them. As they do so, they must be well armed (protected) for the task. Just so Messiah will exercise judgment and will root out evil ones from His kingdom and will cast them into the fire at the final judgment of the ungodly (Matt. 13:30; cf. Mal. 4:1; Rev. 19:15).

E. Catalog of David's Mighty Men (23:8–39)

This catalog is to be compared with 1 Chronicles 11:11–41, where it is indicated that these men helped David win the throne and capture Zion. Three groups appear here, two groups of three (Jashobeam, Eleazar, Shammah; Abishai, Benaiah, one not named); and a group of thirty-one. Twelve of these were appointed commanders of the twelve divisions of the army (1 Chron. 27). Another way of computing the thirty-seven (23:39) is to list three in the first group, two in the second, and thirty-two in the third. Thirty-two are found by changing verse 34 to agree with 1 Chronicles 11:35–36, for Eliphelet read Eliphal and Hepher. Joab is not named, either because he was in a class all by himself as supreme commander, or because he fell from David's favor at the end of his reign. In 1 Chronicles 11:41–47 sixteen additional names appear; possibly they took the place of original members of the group who died and had to be replaced.

Jashobeam (probably the correct reading, adopted from Chronicles, 1 Chron. 27:2), chief of the first group, threw his spear again and again so as to killl eight hundred in one battle (23:8). Eleazar fought with great heroism in a battle against the Philistines. When others retreated, he stood his ground and fought until his hand froze to the sword, i.e., until his muscles became so stiff he could not relax them (23:10). After he had put the enemy to flight by himself, the other Israelites returned to plunder the slain on the battlefield. In another battle against the Philistines, Shammah stood his ground all alone in the middle of the field after the Israelites fled; and God brought about a great victory through him (23:12).

Comments are made on heroes of the second class in verses 18–23. Abishai, brother of Joab, killed over three hundred with his spear in a single battle. He was held in greater honor than the thirty (23:19) and became their commander, though he was not included among them. Benaiah, son of Jehoiada the priest according to 1 Chronicles 27:5, was captain of the Kerethites and Pelethites, David's bodyguard (2 Sam. 8:18; 20:23). He killed two Moabite heroes, a lion in a cistern after it had been driven from its usual habitat by a snowfall, and an Egyptian of great height who possibly was one of the tall Nilotes of East Africa (23:20–21). He was held in higher regard than the Thirty but was not ranked among the top three (23:23).

Since the Thirty are merely named, they require no further comment here, but an anecdote concerning three unnamed members of the group appears in verses 13–17. During one of the conflicts with the Philistines, David longed for a drink of water from the well or cistern at Bethlehem. This was probably more a result of homesickness or frustration than an appreciation of superior water quality. This event apparently took place before David was king, because he was in the cave of Adullam and the Philistines had a garrison at Bethlehem. Desiring to do something kind for their leader, three of the Thirty made their way through the Philistine lines to Bethlehem at the risk of their lives and brought back the desired water. Since drinking this water was almost like drinking the blood of the men who had risked their lives to get it, David refused to drink it and poured it out on the ground as a thank offering to God for the safe return of the three.

F. Census and Plague (24:1–25)

At some time after David's conquests of adjoining kingdoms, and presumably as part of or preparatory to the more complete organization of the administration of Israel during the latter part of his reign, David called for a complete census of his people (cf. 1 Chron. 21). Since a census was not wrong in itself (cf. Exod. 30:12), the sin that was judged in the present case must have been the attitude of the king's heart, and punishment for David's sin then became an occasion for the chastisement of the nation for its waywardness. "Again the anger of the LORD burned against Israel" (24:1) as it had in the days of protracted drought (2 Sam. 21), but the reason is not directly stated in this narrative. In His anger God "moved" (24:1 KJV) or "incited" David to take a census, according to this passage. But God cannot tempt anyone to sin (James 1:13), and the parallel passage in 1 Chronicles 21:1 says that God permitted David to fall into temptation by failing to provide restraining grace.

In what sense David's taking of a census was sinful has to be deduced from the context in 1 Chronicles and 2 Samuel and especially from Joab's response. That David's attitude was sinful certainly is to be seen in his pride, or self-exaltation, as he sought to glory in the number of his fighting men and the strength of his military establishment. And perhaps, worse, he fell to the temptation of measuring his real strength in terms of human and material resources instead of the "Rock" and "Shield" of chapter 22. Joab responded, in effect, that if David had such great delight in numbers, he wished that God would greatly multiply the troops and that the king would live to see it.

The census clearly concerned only the Israelites ("tribes of Israel from Dan to Beersheba" 24:2) and did not include the subject peoples in the empire. And clearly the enrollment was for military rather than taxation or social purposes because it concerned the "fighting men" (24:2 NIV). Moreover, Joab and his subordinates were to take the census. Joab remonstrated with the king, evidently because he felt the king was on an "ego trip" (v. 3), and probably because he believed that any effort to take a census would unsettle the populace, as it would raise fears of new taxes and military conscription. No amount of remonstrance on the part of Joab and the military council was of any avail, however; and the king had his way.

Obediently Joab and the army commanders went off to take the census. Their route was roughly circular, beginning with a stop at Aroer on the north bank of the Arnon River in Trans Jordan, working their way northward on the east side of the Jordan, thence to Dan in the far north, and southward adjacent to southern Lebanon and the non-Israelite holdings along the Mediterranean. Eventually they reached Beersheba in the south and then proceeded northward to Jerusalem. The whole process took nine months and twenty days. Evidently the method was to set up camp in various places ("camped at Aroer," v. 5), and to enroll the men as they reported to the census station. Presumably the compliance was virtually 100 percent because there was little place to hide in an agricultural society and penalties for noncompliance were severe. Moreover, this was merely an enrollment; a threat to report for active duty did not seem to be imminent.

The report separated the census returns for Israel and Judah, revealing a continued tendency to division in the nation. Moreover, the returns recorded in 2 Samuel differed from those given in 1 Chronicles 21:5. Figures given in the former are 800,000 for Israel and 500,000 for Judah; in the latter, 1,100,000 for Israel and 470,000 for Judah. The tendency of many textual critics is to discount so completely the accuracy of numbers in the Bible that they assume errors in cases like this. There are ways to account for the differences, however. For example, the 30,000 commanded by the thirty heroes (1 Chron. 11:25) may be included in Judah in

Samuel but not in 1 Chronicles 21:5; and the 288,000 of the regular army (1 Chron. 27:1–15) may be included in Israel in 1 Chronicles but not in 2 Samuel. Or Chronicles may include resident aliens in the figure for Israel. Other methods of reconciliation have been suggested.

Another problem connected with the census figures is the large numbers they require in the total population—some would say six million. Actually the population of the area exceeds that figure today, and ruins of an abundance of ancient towns dot the region. Moreover, with the shorter life span in ancient times, a larger percentage of the population may have consisted of men of military age. Thus the total population might not have needed to be so large as is sometimes projected.

Evidently, soon after the census was completed, David realized he had done a very foolish thing. Conscience-smitten, he prayed to God for forgiveness. During the night God responded by delivering a message to the prophet Gad who was directed to communicate it to David. As a punishment the king was given a choice of seven years of famine, three months of pursuit before his enemies, and three days of pestilence. All would humble the pride and diminish the resources of the king. Knowing that God was merciful, David chose the last of the three alternatives. Also, conscious of his own sin in bringing on the judgment, David chose to expose himself equally with his people to the punishment. In famine he had resources to guarantee a supply of food; in warfare he had many to protect him; in plague he was equally vulnerable with his people.

So the virulent plague descended. "From the morning until the time designated" (24:15), commonly taken to mean until the time of evening sacrifice (about 3:00 P.M.), seventy thousand "men" (presumably of combat age) died. At that point, on the first day instead of the third, God "repented" (24:16 KJV; "relented," NASB); God changed His attitude toward men because of their changed attitude toward Him. The plague must have been terrible to kill so many in such a short time; that very fact helped to establish it as a supernatural act.

Moreover, the angel that evidently brought the plague was clearly visible to some at least. David saw him by the threshing floor of Araunah the Jebusite, just north of the walled city of Jerusalem. The fact that God stayed the hand of the angel there is an indication that at least the citadel of Jerusalem was spared all effects of the plague. As David saw the terrifying specter of the angel of death, he offered a substitutionary sacrifice, himself and his house: "Let your hand fall upon me and my family" (v. 17 NIV).

God responded with a command through the prophet Gad to build an altar on the threshing floor of Araunah, a descendant of one of the original Jebusite inhabitants of the city. David acted promptly and sought to buy the floor. Though it was customary for an Oriental to offer to give the desired property at an early stage in the negotiation process, though not really intending to do so, in this case the owner may indeed have offered the property to hasten the end of the plague. In any case David rightly concluded that it would be no sacrifice at all to offer up something that cost him nothing, for worship is an expression of a person's giving of his own to God. So he paid an agreed price and made burnt offerings (expiatory) and peace offerings (in thanksgiving for the end of the plague) in the newly established holy place. This passage says David paid fifty shekels of silver for the threshing floor; 1 Chronicles 21:25 states that he paid six hundred shekels of gold "for the site," evidently the large area on which the temple later would be built. Second Chronicles 3:1 makes it clear that the threshing floor of Araunah was on the northeast hill of Jerusalem, which was also Mount Moriah, the place where Abraham offered Isaac (Gen. 22:2).

Conclusion

Just as 1 Samuel stops almost in the middle of a thought, so 2 Samuel (though it has a convenient end with its appendices, chaps. 21–24) concludes in an inconvenient place—just short of the end of David's life (1 Kings 2:10–11). As noted before the Septuagint translation calls for four books of Samuel and Kings the books of "The Kingdoms." In them the story is told of kingship in Israel, beginning with Saul and continuing through the reigns of David and Solomon in the united monarchy, and on through the history of the divided kingdom until Israel is swallowed up by foreign powers.

Clearly, true monarchy was established in the figure of David and continued in the long line of his descendants. Though that line was to be interrupted, it was to have an eternal aspect fulfilled in the person of the Messiah. Only the Messiah could fulfill the eternal aspects of the Davidic covenant (2 Sam. 7), and foregleams of His rule occur in such passages as David's last words (2 Sam. 23:1–7).

Also, Zadok appears on the scene in 2 Samuel as the head of a priestly line that comes to be regarded as the legitimate priesthood of Jerusalem. The true shrine of Israel also is introduced. David captures Jerusalem and establishes it as the capital. His desire to build a proper house for God there is met by the assurance that it will be built by his son. He gathers materials for the temple and ultimately buys the spot on which it is to be constructed from Araunah the Jebusite.

Attention in these two books focuses especially on David, who in Acts 13:22 is called a man after God's own heart. Many sneer at the description and ask how it can be so when he was guilty of adultery and murder. The answer must lie first in the consideration of the context. Saul had been disobedient; in his public policies he had failed God and later had even sought to kill God's anointed (David). Therefore, God had rejected him. This same point is made in 1 Samuel 13:13–14: Saul did not honor God in his public policies; so God sought out a man after His own heart to lead His people.

David always was faithful to God in his public pronouncements and actions. He respected the anointed of God (Saul) and refused to kill him even under the greatest duress. In his early warfare, which is all that is described in any detail, he sought God's instruction about going into battle. He made the sanctuary of God prominent in Jerusalem at the center of the affairs of state and sought to build a house for God. When denied the privilege, he amassed quantities of precious metals for the purpose instead of collecting them for himself as other Oriental potentates did. He organized the worship of Israel and honored God in prayer in the presence of the whole assembly (1 Chron. 29:10–13). Moreover, he wrote many psalms, some of which were adapted for the ritual of public worship.

Second, David was a man after God's own heart even in his private or inner life. He meditated on the Word of God and generally had a beautiful devotional life, as the psalms he wrote indicate. To be sure he sinned and sinned grievously, and he paid dearly for his failures. But what matters especially is what he did about his sins. He had a heart tender toward God. When he realized his sins or was confronted with them, he demonstrated a broken and a contrite heart and sought God's forgiveness. It must be remembered that he lived before the cross, before there was a canon of Scripture, and before the permanent indwelling of the Holy Spirit in the believer. His was the faithful struggle of an earnest human soul to know God. Even though he suffered shipwreck as he sailed the seas of life, by the grace of God he never went down for the third time. Modern believers may identify with him as they struggle against heavy seas, and by grace they may experience the same rescuing and sustaining hand of God.

For Further Study

1. From David's psalm in chapter 22, work out a statement of his concept of God. What attributes or characteristics of God can you identify?

2. What is the meaning and significance of the reference to Jesus Christ as the Son of David? Consult a Bible dictionary or encyclopedia.

3. What additional information on the life and character of David may be gleaned from 1 Kings 1:1–2:11?

4. As you think through David's life, which of his character traits stand out most and why?

Bibliography

Ackroyd, Peter R. *The First Book of Samuel.* Cambridge: At the University Press, 1971.

——————. *The Second Book of Samuel.* Cambridge: At the Univeristy Press, 1977.

Archer, Gleason L. *A Survey of Old Testament Introduction*, rev. ed. Chicago: Moody, 1974.

Blaikie, W. G. *First and Second Samuel* in *The Expositor's Bible*, vol. 2. Grand Rapids: Eerdmans, 1943.

Crockett, William D. *A Harmony of Samuel, Kings, and Chronicles.* New York: Eaton & Mains, 1897.

Hertzberg, Hans W. *I and II Samuel.* Philadelphia: Westminster, 1964.

Jamieson, Robert; Fausset, Andrew R.; and Brown, David. *A Commentary, Critical, Experimental, and Practical on the Old and New Testaments.* Grand Rapids: Eerdmans, 1945 reprint.

Keil, C. F., and Delitzsch, F. *Biblical Commentary on the Books of Samuel.* Edinburgh: T & T Clark, n. d.

Larey, J. Carl. *First and Second Samuel.* Chicago: Moody, 1982.

Meyer, F. B. *David: Shepherd, Psalmist, King.* London: Morgan and Scott, n. d.

Renwick, A. M., "I and II Samuel," *New Bible Commentary.* Edited by F. Davidson and others. Grand Rapids: Eerdmans, rev. ed., 1954.

Ridout, Samuel. *King Saul.* New York: Bible Truth, n. d.

Smith, Henry P. *A Critical and Exegetical Commentary on the Books of Samuel.* New York: Charles Scribner's Sons, 1899.

Unger, Merrill F. *Biblical Demonology*, 2nd ed. Wheaton: Van Kampen, 1953.

Wood, Leon J. *Israel's United Monarchy.* Grand Rapids:Baker, 1979.

——————. *A Survey of Israel's History.* Grand Rapids: Zondervan, 1970.

Whyte, Alexander. *Bible Characters*. Edinburgh: Oliphants, n.d.
Young, Fred E. "I and II Samuel," *The Wycliffe Bible Commentary*. Edited by Charles Pfeiffer and Everett F. Harrison. Chicago: Moody, 1962.

Listed below are Bible translations specifically referred to in this study.

The Jerusalem Bible. Garden City, N.Y.: Doubleday, 1966. Referred to in this study as JB.

New American Standard Bible. La Habra, Calif.: Lockman Foundation, 1960. Referred to in this study as NASB.

The New English Bible. Oxford: University Press, 1970. Referred to in this study as NEB.

New International Version. New York: New York Bible Society, 1978. Referred to in this study as NIV.

The Holy Bible. The Authorized or King James Version. Referred to in this study as KJV.

The Holy Bible. The Revised Standard Version. New York: Thomas Nelson & Sons, 1946. Referred to in this study as RSV.